TO DOD

FROM ONE CULTURE TO
ANOTHER!

Y.S

Peter McKendrie

This book is dedicated in loving memory of my son Tony Tunkals Albert (Bones) Harrison (6.9.1960-14.3.2000) who now sits with the wisdom of the ancestors.

An Aboriginal Elder
speaks on life, land,
spirit and forgiveness

Max Dulumunmun Harrison

Featuring photographs and recordings by Peter McConchie

FINCH PUBLISHING

SYDNEY

In memory of those gone by

Where are the faces that once smiled with pride
Or they sometimes just talked of respect.
They would feed you and give you a bed for the night
Or they told you to never neglect.

To never abandon your duties to teach
Or never let go of your laws.
Never to think that today became hard
Or life's full of some difficult chores.

I reflect to the Forties and Fifties, then more
To the Sixties when folks used to meet
In the paddocks while picking the peas and the beans
Or sometimes we would meet on the street.

But something went wrong when they opened the doors
Of the gambling clubs and the bars
The grog and the gambling soon took its toll
Leaving loved ones with spiritual scars.

Not only spiritual scars did they bear
There was mental and physical pain.
Some joined the ancients in that spiritual world
While some never recovered again.

So those faces that smiled
Or they held out their hands
To welcome you into the fold
They are no longer there in that physical form
But are there for our thoughts to behold.

Max Dulumunmun Harrison

CONTENTS

Seeing the Land   7

Begin with Mother Earth 9
Yuin country 13
Gulaga Mountain and the Creation Dreaming 17
Songlines 33
Grandfather Sun 41
Koorah Koo-rie wind spirit 47
Reading the land 51
The seasons 55
The three principles of learning 59
The truth of traditional knowledge 67
My teachers 71
Our laws and punishment 79
Totems 87
Skin names 91
Sacred places 95
Barran-guba Island 99
Initiation 105
Death and burial 115
Communicating with the dead 119
Ceremony 123
Whale Elders 129
Boundaries and borders 133
Singing tree 139
Food as medicine 145
Forgiveness 151

Acknowledgements 158
A note from Peter McConchie 159

SEEING THE LAND

In this book I am trying to raise awareness of Aboriginal spirituality and to explain how we connect to the land. I am trying to capture in words the beauty of the land I see around me. And seeing is so important … really seeing what the land is telling you. Seeing what the land is offering for you to take.

When I take people out into the land I say: 'Let's watch the land talk to us.' And you'll see some jaws drop. But that's what it's doin' – it's talking to us without a voice.

Our land does that all the time; our water does that, our wind. Grandmother Moon, Grandfather Sun do it all the time. They show us things, what's happening. They are talking to us constantly. And what do we do? We ignore them; we ignore what the Mother, the land, is telling us. We don't do the ceremony we used to do, we don't sing in the trees when we plant them, we don't see which direction the songlines are taking. We just rip down trees or plant them willy-nilly. And we wonder why the rains don't come to the trees.

The teachings I reveal in this book are the living treasures of my life. The traditional knowledge I talk about includes Creation Dreaming, bush lore, foods and healing, laws and punishment, spirituality and relationship to the land. These are some of the things taught to me by my teachers, my masters. And I will never forget them. They made me look at the Mother with ancient eyes. Not mine. But with ancient eyes. And now it is my turn to pass on what I know.

Begin with Mother Earth

"Mother Earth births everything for us. Father Sky carries the water and oxygen for us to breathe. Grandfather Sun warms the planet, warms our body, gives us light so we can see, raises the food that the Mother births and raises most of our relations, all our plants and trees. Grandmother Moon moves the water and gives us the woman-time and our birthing."

Grandmother Moon, she comes up and shines down her light upon us. She pulls the tides of the sea. She has that much strength she can pull water up into the sky and hold it, until it's time to water her garden, Mother Earth.

Mother Earth, Father Sky, Grandmother Moon and Grandfather Sun have the major roles to play in all life. Water is connected to Mother Earth and to Father Sky. Water is also connected to Grandmother Moon, as she can lift the water and drop it down through Father Sky. Mother Earth then takes the water and she distributes it through her rivers, streams and lakes.

Father Sky holds many stories; through time he has led the way for us to navigate over water and land. He's there for us, he helps us find our way.

Yuin Country

"Our Dreaming starts up near Braidwood and Majors Creek, my great-grandmother and grandmother's country. As the Shoalhaven River winds around and bends, it brings with it all the different stories from the different parts of the river. The river leads us to the sea, and shows us that we are freshwater and saltwater water people. If we didn't follow the stories that the Shoalhaven River brings us we would not be able to find our way down to the sea and to our homeland."

Yuin country, my people's land, extends from the Snowy River in the south to the escarpment of Wollongong, our northern boundary, and then out on to the Southern Tablelands. Our country follows the coast down and into Victoria. It is our home; we camp and live here.

The Shoalhaven River is part of our Dreaming. The Dreaming is like a pathway. The pathway is made up stories of different events, like initiations and ceremonies, that have happened on particular parts of the river, up and down the river you know, whichever way the Dreaming was going.

The Dreaming runs from Braidwood. Braidwood is my great-grandmother and grandmother's country. The Dreaming that comes down towards Nowra is called the Gadu Dreaming. Gadu is the ocean. Of course, all the water runs into the ocean and we follow that Dreaming and those stories that come down the river, and that's why it's respected as the Dreaming track.

We have other Dreaming tracks that go across land: some follow the rivers down, some go over ridges and mountains ... wherever that Dreaming will go.

This is the Shoalhaven River part of Yuin country, my people's land. It is wonderful to be here by this beautiful river that holds so much memory of my culture. This river is a journey that leads from the mountains to the sea. It's a place of sacred walking. Some of the areas of the river are stronger than others, such as the bend in the river, the branches that feed off it and those creeks that feed into the main body of the river. These are powerful and significant to our people. There may be ceremony performed at any of these places.

Gulaga Mountain and the Creation Dreaming

"When we walk onto Gulaga Mountain we walk into sacredness. Every time I go there it gives me a spiritual uplifting and I learn more about how our people were created. I realise how important it is that I show Gulaga to as many different people as I can and explain our Creation Story so our heritage is not ignored. I never tire of going to Gulaga."

Gulaga Mountain is where the Creation Story begins for the people of the Yuin Nation, my people. Gulaga [*Mt Dromedary*] is in Gulaga National Park on the far south coast of New South Wales. Gulaga gives us our stories of Creation. Gulaga gives us our stories of connectedness with the other clan groups that are scattered within the Yuin Nation. Up on Gulaga there are many rocks or tors that form a straight line and each one tells part of the story of all things. Each tor is a chapter in our Creation Story.

Previous page: Walking into sacredness on Gulaga Mountain.
Left: The Rainbow Serpent, one of the sacred rocks on Gulaga Mountain. Gulaga is near Narooma, on the south coast of New South Wales.

The first rock of connectedness, the Creation Rock.

The story starts with the first rock of connectedness; we call this the Energy Rock or Creation Rock.

This rock tells how Daramah, the Great Spirit, created the heavens and the earth and all nature. Then Daramah created two people. First he created a woman and he called her Ngardi (pronounced Nardi with a soft g, as in song). The next creation was a man and his name was Tunku. This is not like the Bible when it was Adam who was the first one created, then Eve next. That's not like our stories.

These two rocks, Ngardi and Tunku, are placed either side from the Creation Rock. Then Daramah, Great Creator, gave Ngardi and Tunku two gifts. And the two gifts were a rock and a tree. The rock and the tree symbolise everything that they would use for their survival. Daramah's words to Ngardi and Tunku were: 'You will take these two gifts and use what you get from them. And they will become sacred to you in your lore that you hand down to the offspring. To the coming generation.'

Ngardi

Tunku

The rock and the tree that Daramah gave Ngardi and Tunku.

But what good is a rock and a tree? Well, the rocks hold water for us. People might think: 'How could the rock hold water?' But look at the modern structure of rocks that are put into dams to hold the water that is brought down the creeks, so that us lazy, good for nothings, all we do is get out of bed, walk into our bathroom, and turn a tap and we've got water that instant. What brings that water to us? Rocks, you see.

The old system of connecting back to these two gifts is one part of that rock. The next part is the tree, which helps with the structure of giving you shelter. It also gives you medicines and oxygen, and foods. Ngardi and Tunku had to start their observation program of watching the trees and the rocks and seeing what could be done with them.

And then they found out that they could get warmth and light from the tree, and also from the rocks by using the flint, or rubbing the two sticks together and creating the fires. They can use all the materials from a tree for their shelter. Making the bark humpies out of the trees. They could use medicines within the barks and the leaves. That's why Daramah gave only those two gifts to Ngardi and Tunku.

Why was Ngardi the first creation of the human race? Simple. Because Ngardi was the one that could give birth. I've never seen a man give birth to a child. That is the basis of the respect Law for the woman.

Next in the Creation Story are three rocks that sit on top of each other. The first one on the bottom represents where we come from, that we come from the land. The next one that sits on top of it tells us where we are now.

The third one is a tall one pointing toward the heavens, and it shows us that's where we go when our spirit leaves our body and passes into the next world. But the one in the middle is the one that is important for us. It shows us we're between love and hate, that we're between hot and cold, that we're between hunger and fullness, between evil and greatness. It shows us and tells us how important it is to live each day at a time. That's very important on Gulaga, that part of the chapter.

When we take people on tours to Gulaga and we get to Creation Rock, we ask for healing for different things, different hurts. And after each healing that we do we ask Koorah Koo-rie wind spirit to come and take away our healing. I've learnt over the 20-odd years of going up on the mountain to ask for gentle winds. I used to just always say: 'Now I'll ask Koorah Koo-rie wind spirit to come and blow our healing,' and oh boy, we'd either get wet or drenched. And then I started to think, 'Hang on, I'm asking for these things, and I'm getting them.' So then I learnt to change my language, and I learnt to start to ask Koorah Koo-rie wind spirit to come and gently blow on us.

Some people that have been on the mountain with me a couple of times say, 'Gee, that was good. You can say that now without us getting wet.' And I'd say, 'Yes, but did you notice the change in my language? I said "gently blow".'

The three rocks that sit on top of one another. These rocks are one of the most valuable things about Gulaga to me. When I am in trouble in my mind, body or spirit, my mind goes straight to these rocks. They show me where I come from, where I am now and where I am going to in the spirit world.

Next we have another great rock to attend to, which is the pregnant mother, the pregnant woman. And that pregnant woman shows us that we must always respect our mother. We must always respect our women.

Just beside that mother is another little rock which is one of the nurses or the helpers for that pregnancy, the 'midwife' you would call her in English terms. And around that little rock were some plants that helped with childbirth and pregnancy. But someone showed some people the particular beautiful little plants, and told them a little bit about it. And then the plants were taken; probably to be grown somewhere else for profit.

But the minute that you take that plant, the rest of it all just dies. The ancient knowledge should stay there. When the ancients used it they only took part of a leaf to help with childbirth. Now it never grows back, won't grow back. I know where there's more, just a bit more. But now I can't even show that to anyone. So I'm going to die with that knowledge of where that plant is now, 'cause now I don't know who I can trust with some of that sacred knowledge.

The next rock we come to is the Birthing Rock. After every pregnancy comes the birthing, and there's a child, which you'll see being nurtured and carried. So you see this little baby [*boori*] sitting on its mother's hip being carried until it is old enough to go onto the next rock.

Previous page: The pregnant woman.
Left: The Boori Rock.

Then the next tor or rock is the Teaching Rock. It is where you go to learn. We call it the 'school' or the 'high school' because it's high. From there you'll look down and see the first group of big totems: the Whale Rock, the Dugong, the Shark and the big fella that's all around the country, the Rainbow Serpent.

Many times I knew people who had fear and I sat them on the edge of the teaching rock and we helped them to remove their fear. It is a dangerous procedure, but one of the most important things to remember is to have faith in your teachings. You must have faith in the spirits that are there to help you and guide you. I have all of the faith because no-one has fallen over the edge yet. I get the people to walk backwards towards the edge gently with their eyes closed and I talk them through it, and the rest of the people sit around and watch in anticipation and you can feel their energies. The rock also teaches the people who are watching when they see the others coming back after their lesson. It feels so good to know that most of them have lost their fears. The Teaching Rock is not just a place of teaching about how the rock holds water, or how the rock is used for making a stone implement like our axes, our knives, it's also a place to teach you how to self-heal your fears.

Top: The Teaching Rock, where you can look down and see all the totems below you.

Bottom right: The Rainbow Serpent, who went underground and created all the rivers. Here he is, coming up to look at all his good work. The story of the Rainbow Serpent is common to all Aboriginal tribes.

Bottom left: The Whale Rock. Can you see him breaching? This rock signifies the whale coming up out of the water to spread his lore so we can understand more about the sea.

As you wind your way down off the Teaching Rock you arrive at one of the great places for removing fear. During every journey down that rock, people are asked to just grab a little pebble or a bit of dirt and carry it down to the Stones of the Future, where we finish our journey, and throw them in there and pay their dues to Gulaga Mountain, sacred mountain. Then, as they do so, I show them some of the other wonderful things that they must learn: that the mountain calls them back, not physically but spiritually and mentally, and they will look back upon their journey and revisit a place of sacredness.

And that's how that story is laid out on that sacred ridge of Gulaga, on that sacred text of the land. Gulaga is sacred because it holds the story of creation of the Yuin Nation. We have been trying to get Gulaga classed in the category of one of the wonders of the world because to the Yuin people that's what it means to us – she is one of the wonders of the world.

Top: The Shark.
Bottom: The Dugong. When I show people from other Aboriginal tribes these totems they almost fall off the Teaching Rock in surprise, because they have these totems in their dreaming too. This shows how connected we are with other people of the northern waters.

SONGLINES

"The songlines are such an important part of our mental and spiritual structure. They are lines of energy that run between places, animals and people. We know at times where the songlines are and we like to follow them for the energy, not only because we can send a message to other neighbouring tribes but so we can keep in touch with animal and bird life. We follow the songlines of the animals to know where they are and to see if they have moved on. If they have moved on then we can start a burn off to create more life without hurting the animals."

Gulaga is our weather forecaster; she lets us know when we're going to get a bit of water from Father Sky. Gulaga is a woman's mountain as much as it is a man's mountain because of the creation of the woman first and the man second. Gulaga is a place of wisdom, a place of tranquillity. Gulaga is also a great place for communicating from the first Creation Rock. From there we can send out messages and connect with the other tribes. Gulaga also oversees her youngest son Nadjinooka [*Little Dromedary*] and her oldest son Barranguba [*Montague Island*], and then her sister mountain, Biamanga [*Mumbulla*]. Biamanga is a place of journey, of learning, and you have to do many walks there to go through the learning period and initiations. Gulaga is a teaching place and a birthing place.

Gulaga is also connecteded to a sacred place up near Whittakers Creek, just north of Narooma, where two young girls ran away with their dogs. By running away they disobeyed the Elders and they were caught up and turned into stone. The stones are in a direct line to where the woman stories are told on Gulaga.

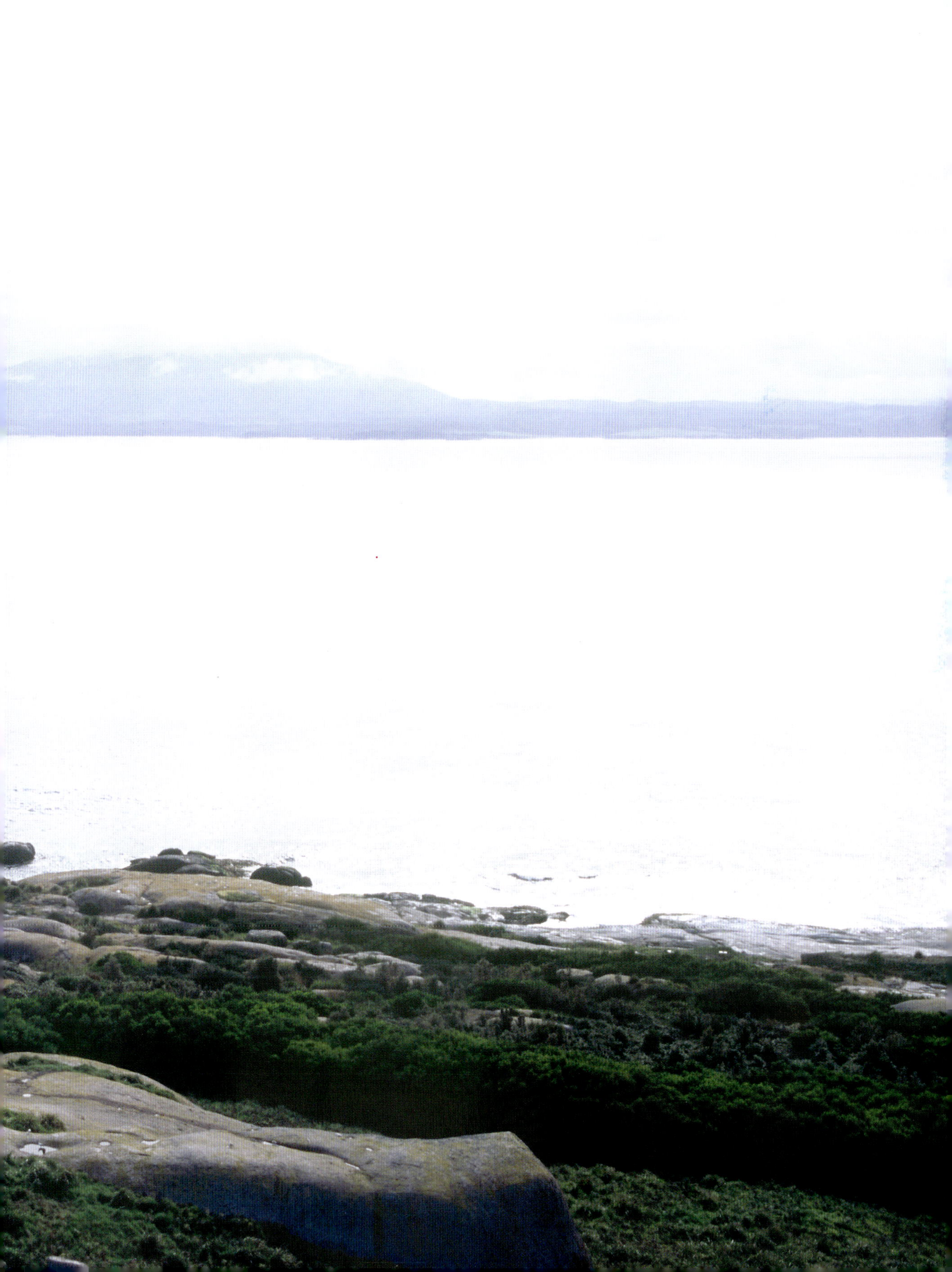

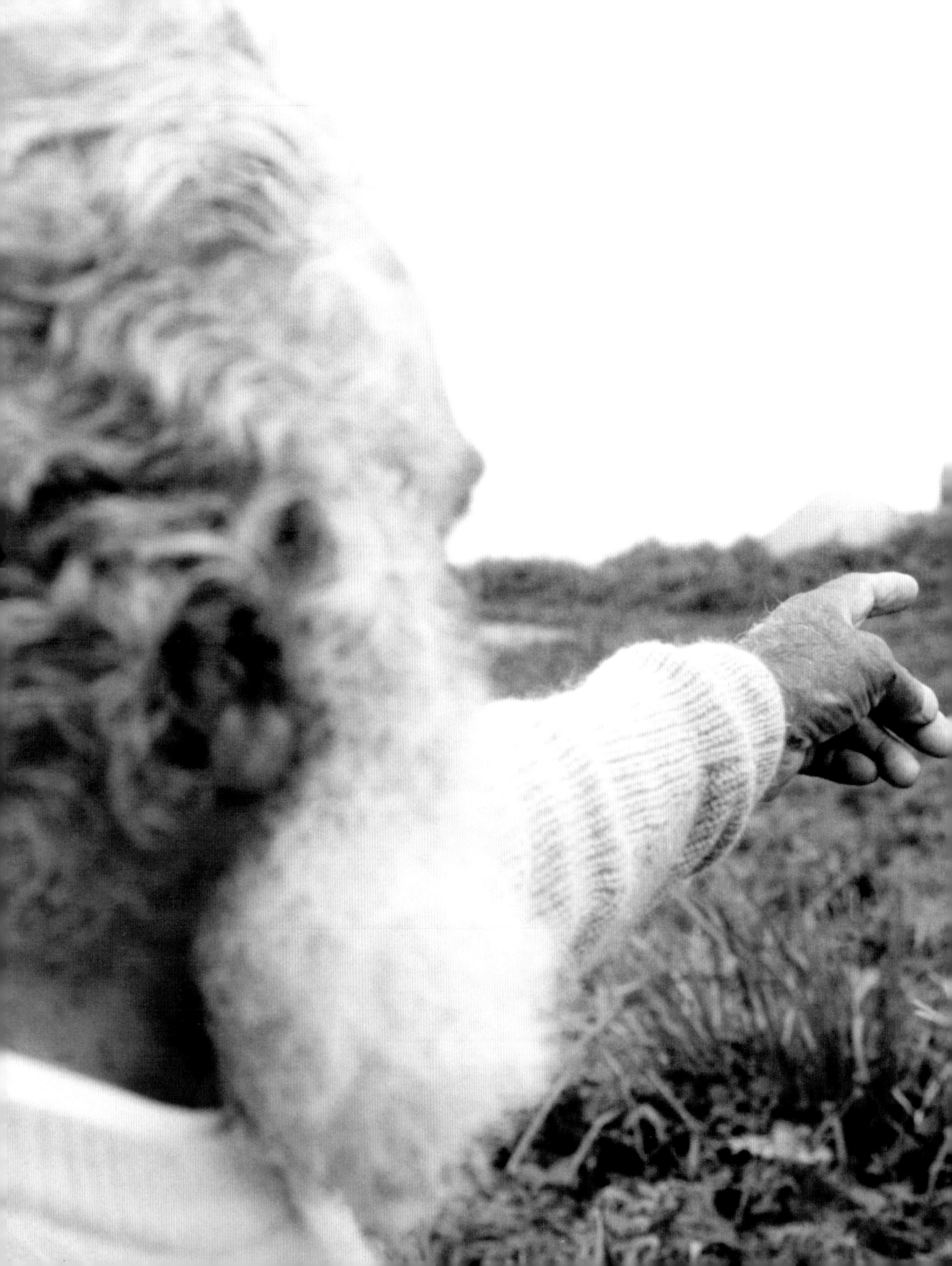

Just a year after the handback of Gulaga and Biamanga to the Yuin people, forestry went in and cut trees down and disrupted the sacred songlines. When I tried to tell them they shouldn't do that because it cut the direct line of teaching, it was disregarded. Forestry just overruled it and they persuaded some Yuin people to give the go-ahead. I was disgusted to even think that some of our mob wouldn't listen; they know the story of the two sisters and our cultural ways and how it is told up on that mountain.

People can't understand about the sacredness and those songlines, those Dreaming lines. They say cutting trees down at the base of the mountain is not touching the sacred sites up top, but they don't understand about the short circuiting of the spiritual connectedness from one place to the other. As you know, when you drive around the country with your talking sticks – your mobile phones – you can get into what you call dead spots, the spots where you are cut off. That is what these people have done in coercing my mob, who don't know the deeper part of the story where the Dreaming travels to. They have cut the songlines. People cannot understand Aboriginal spiritual connectedness and the lines of connectedness. We have heard the comment before of 'We're not logging up on the mountain'. I say, 'Yes, but the base is the strength, how do you think a mountain becomes a mountain? It comes from the bottom up and peaks at the top. If you haven't got a strong base then you can't stand up.'

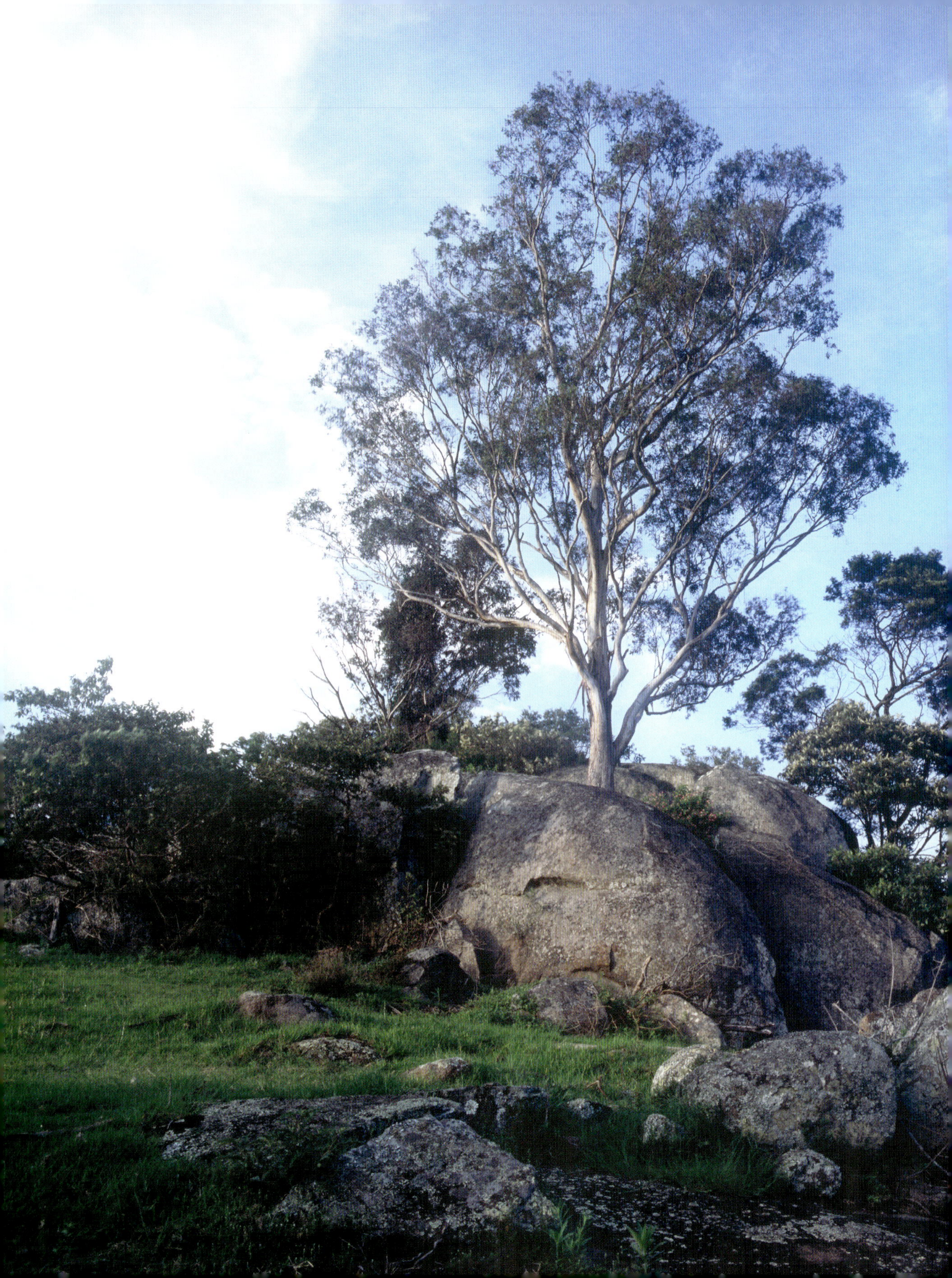

In my 70 and more years, I have never been to the summit on Gulaga. There is no need for me to go that far – my teachings are on that saddle [*ridge*]. So one day when I'm about 80 years of age I might take a toddle up there and take a look at the view. You see I've never looked at the view from Gulaga, I've only looked at the stories that she offered me, only drunk in the spiritual energy that she served to me and only taken the wisdom that was offered to me.

There is plenty in that library up there, it is the text of the land. The library is open, it has its own dictionary to explain the languages spoken there. It has all those wonderful gifts for us to borrow, so we can pass them on. And that's what we must do with our gifts of knowledge when we come down from Gulaga. We must give them away to keep them – and that tells us that we will return to Gulaga, that the mountain will call us back.

Gulaga was never a place to camp or just to visit. As soon as you step up into that sacred area there is no hunting or gathering, not even eating. Clap once as you enter and again when you leave for each person and wear a red headband to show respect for its greatness. It is the place of creation. Take nothing except for its knowledge.

Pages 34 & 35: Gulaga with her 'possum cloak' of cloud, seen from Barran-guba.
Previous page: On Barran-guba, the oldest son of Gulaga Mountain.
Left: At the base of Gulaga. If you haven't got a strong base then you can't stand up.

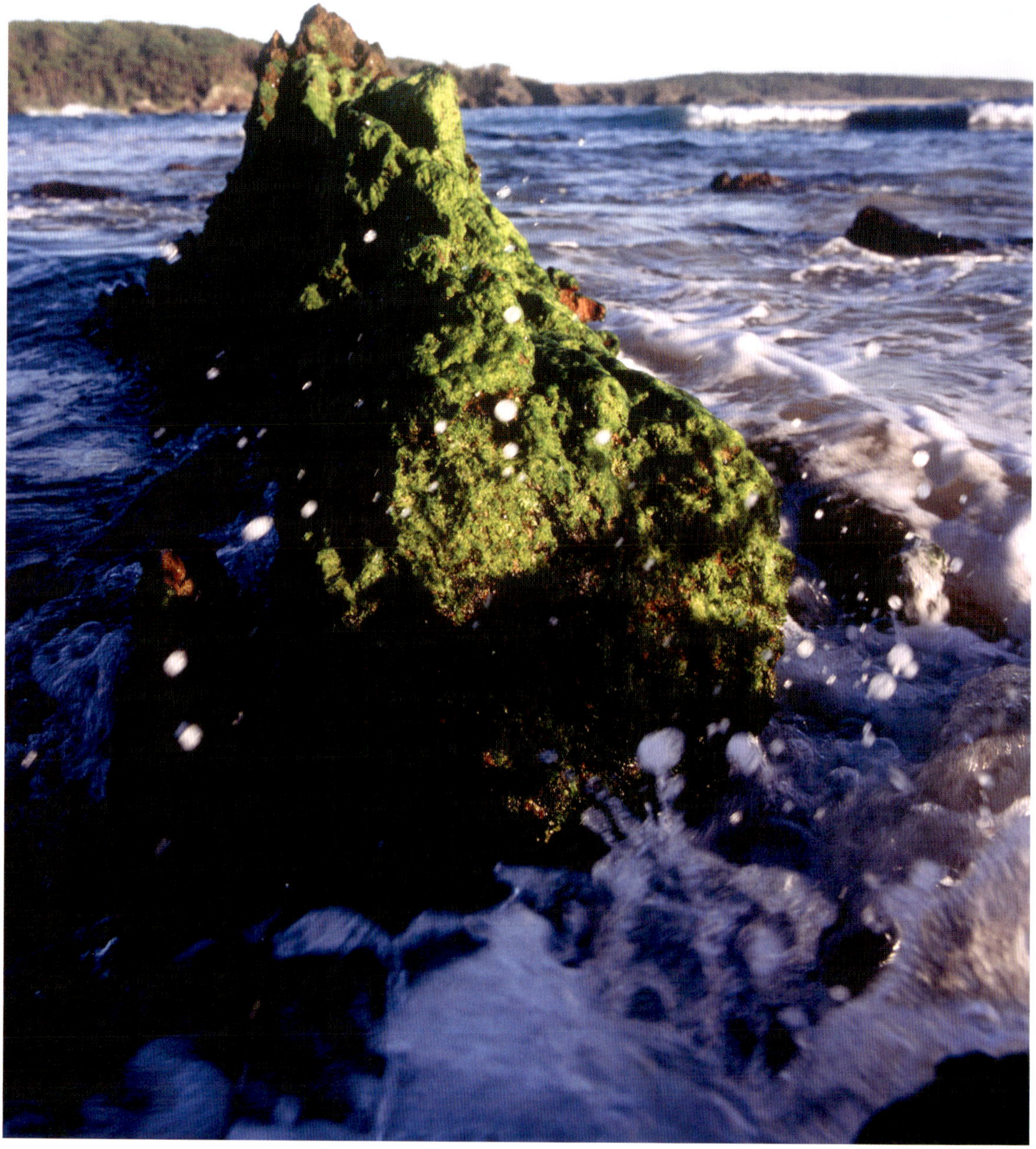

GRANDFATHER SUN

"Grandfather Sun has a big influence on story telling. Even the hot coals in a fire are part of Grandfather Sun. It's the energy of Grandfather Sun that helps create the stories. When we have a campfire, Grandfather Sun is much closer to you and you can invite people in and around him to sit down and look into the flame to tell stories. Someone once said to me: 'Oh, what are you doing telling a story and looking into the fire? That's poor man's television,' and I say, 'Yeah but the story is true.'

When we finish with the fire we cover the coals over with dirt, not water, because it is not right to leave the coals exposed - it can cause damage to the atmosphere. Our mob has been looking after the environment for tens of thousands of years."

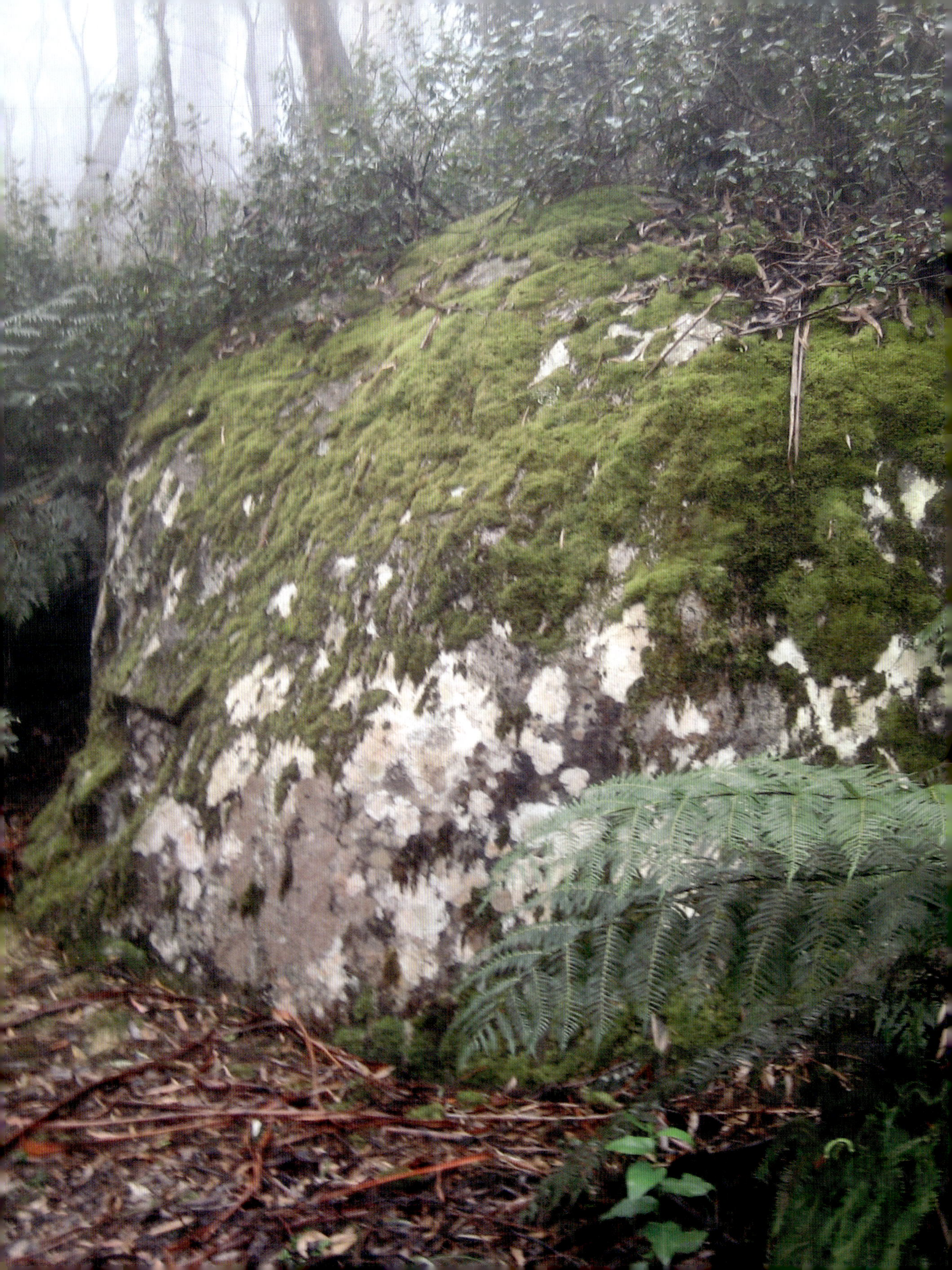

What you call fire I call Grandfather Sun. When I was around nine years old, climbing a tree, my grandfather said to me, 'Dulumunmun, did you get permission from that tree to climb it?'

'No,' I replied.

'Dulumunmun, you should get permission,' he said.

'But this tree is dead,' I said.

He yelled at me to get down, then he never said a word until it was time to eat. Then Grandfather said to me, 'You go and get some of the dead tree for the fire.' So I went and got all these dead sticks and limbs to make the fire.

After the billy was boiled and the damper cooked and we had finished our lunch, Grandfather said to me, 'Dulumunmun, pick up those hot coals.'

I looked at him and said, 'I can't pick them up.'

'Why? They're dead, aren't they?' he asked.

'No, they're alive.' And then I shut up. That's when he told me about Grandfather Sun.

'These coals are still part of Grandfather Sun, and you thought that tree was dead. That tree is part of Grandfather Sun, that bit of black charcoal is holding Grandfather Sun.'

There is that wonderful connectedness from way up there in the sky and here on Mother Earth. In between are Grandmother Moon and Father Sky. Everyday when Grandfather Sun comes up all these little plants and flowers open up to greet him and they welcome him. And that's what we do too, greet Grandfather and pay our respects.

We thank Grandfather for the light and the warmth and for the food that we will eat. He's put his rays upon the earth and risen that food up.

Thanking Grandfather Sun

Thank you for your light,
thank you for your warmth that
you will give me today,
thank you for the food that you
have raised that I will have to eat.

Thank you Grandfather
for the wonderful things
that you have grown, that
Mother Earth has birthed.

Thank you Grandfather
for your communication with
Grandmother Moon which now
sits with you in the sky
and thank you Grandfather
for the life that you give to all
the plants and the animals.

Thank you Grandfather
for everything that you warm
and you heat.
Thank you Grandfather for being there.

And I also thank Daramah,
Great Creator of Mother Earth,
Father Sky, Grandmother Moon and
Grandfather sun.

Thank you Daramah
for your creations
of all the birdlife, of all the fish life,
reptile life
and every living thing that is around us,
and I thank you Daramah, Great Creator,
for the creation of our people.
Natcha tong Nungha (to the Mother).

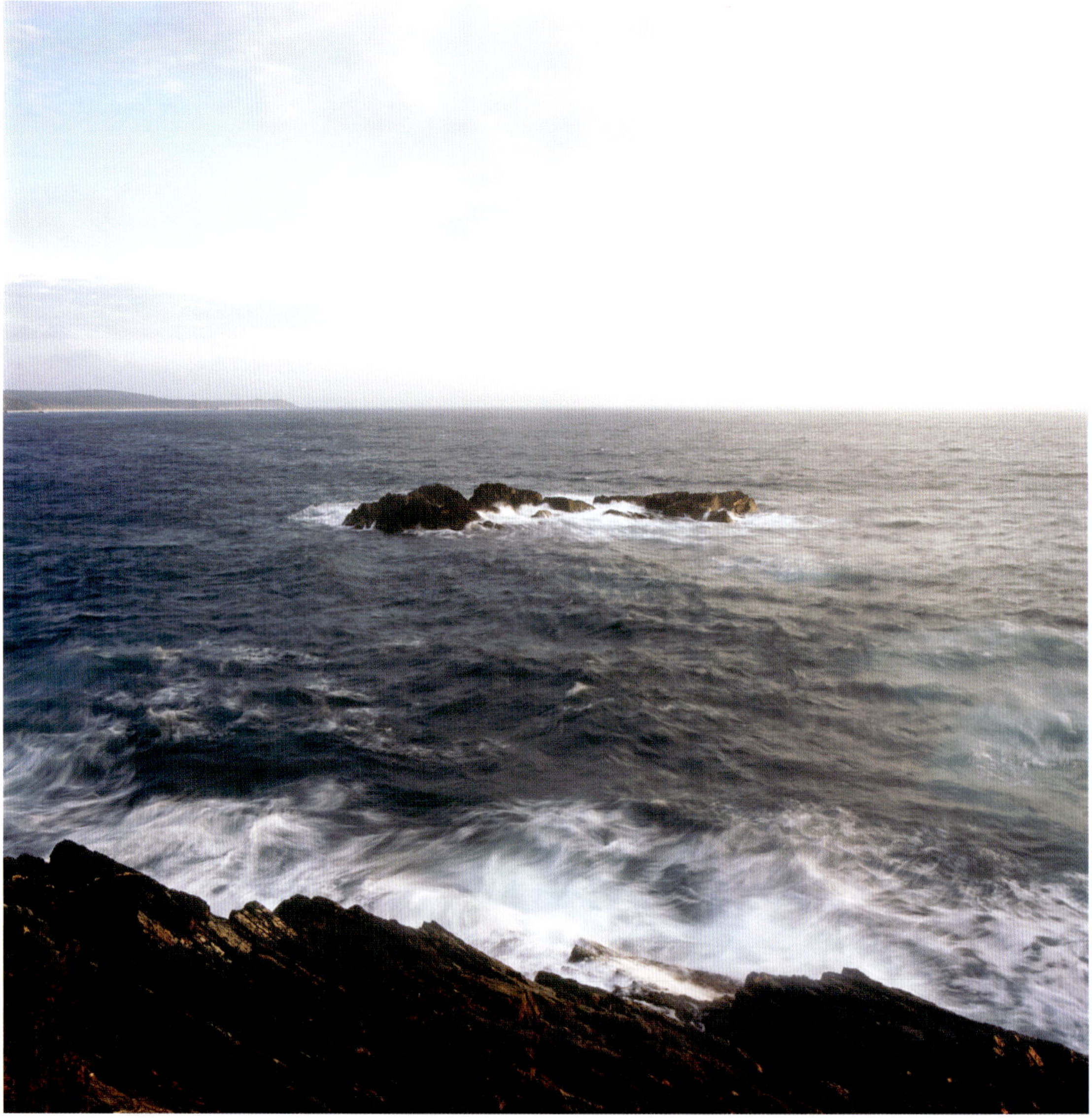

KOORAH KOO-RIE WIND SPIRIT

"Here you can see the work of Koorah Koo-rie, the wind spirit. We must respect the power of Koorah Koo-rie at all times. We can call on Koorah Koo-rie just like we can call on water and fire when it is necessary to change the weather pattern. We held as many wind dances as we did rain and fire dances."

Koorah Koo-rie wind spirit comes in from all directions; each season calls in its favoured direction. In the summer time when Grandfather Sun is closer to us we looked forward to Koorah Koo-rie wind spirit to come from the south and cool us down.

When Koorah Koo-rie wind spirit is coming from the west over to our eastern seaboard, my Uncles would know and go over to the beaches to sing up that west wind for it to blow offshore. Then they could see the waves and throw their nets; they would catch five or six big fish, enough for a feast. Mother Earth guided us, telling us where we should be.

When I ask people, 'What's your favourite wind?' their jaws drop and they say, 'What do you mean?' Okay, what would you prefer on a stinking hot day – a hot westerly or a north-easterly or a good cold southerly buster to cool everything down? And so that's how you start to recognise your winds and start to understand the power of Koorah Koo-rie. Then you can call on Koorah Koo-rie to come and change the situation of the weather pattern. Koorah Koo-rie is one of the touchiest spirits that you can call on.

A cliff face at Mystery Bay, near Narooma, New South Wales. You can see the power of Koorah Koo-rie wind spirit at work here.

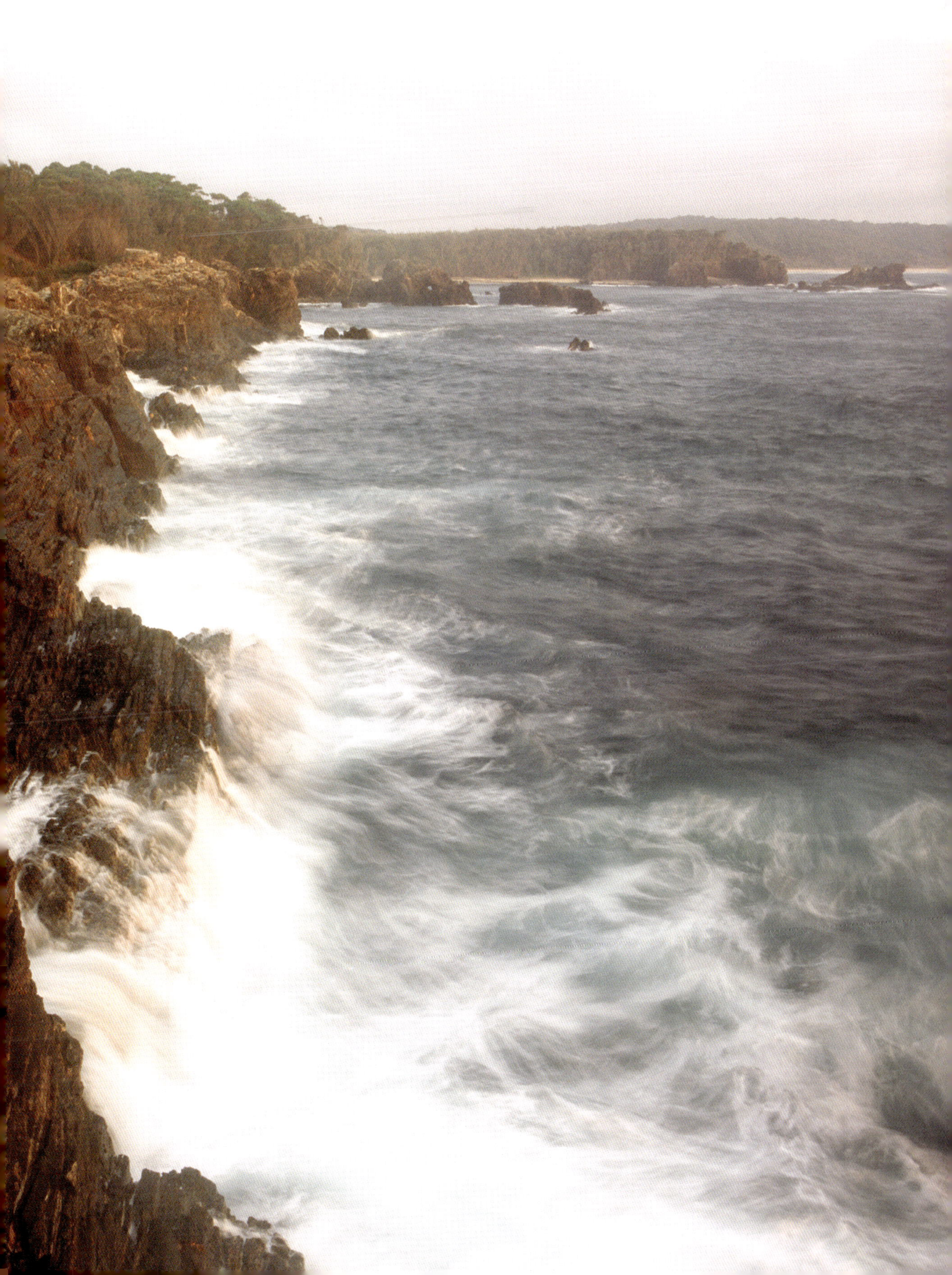

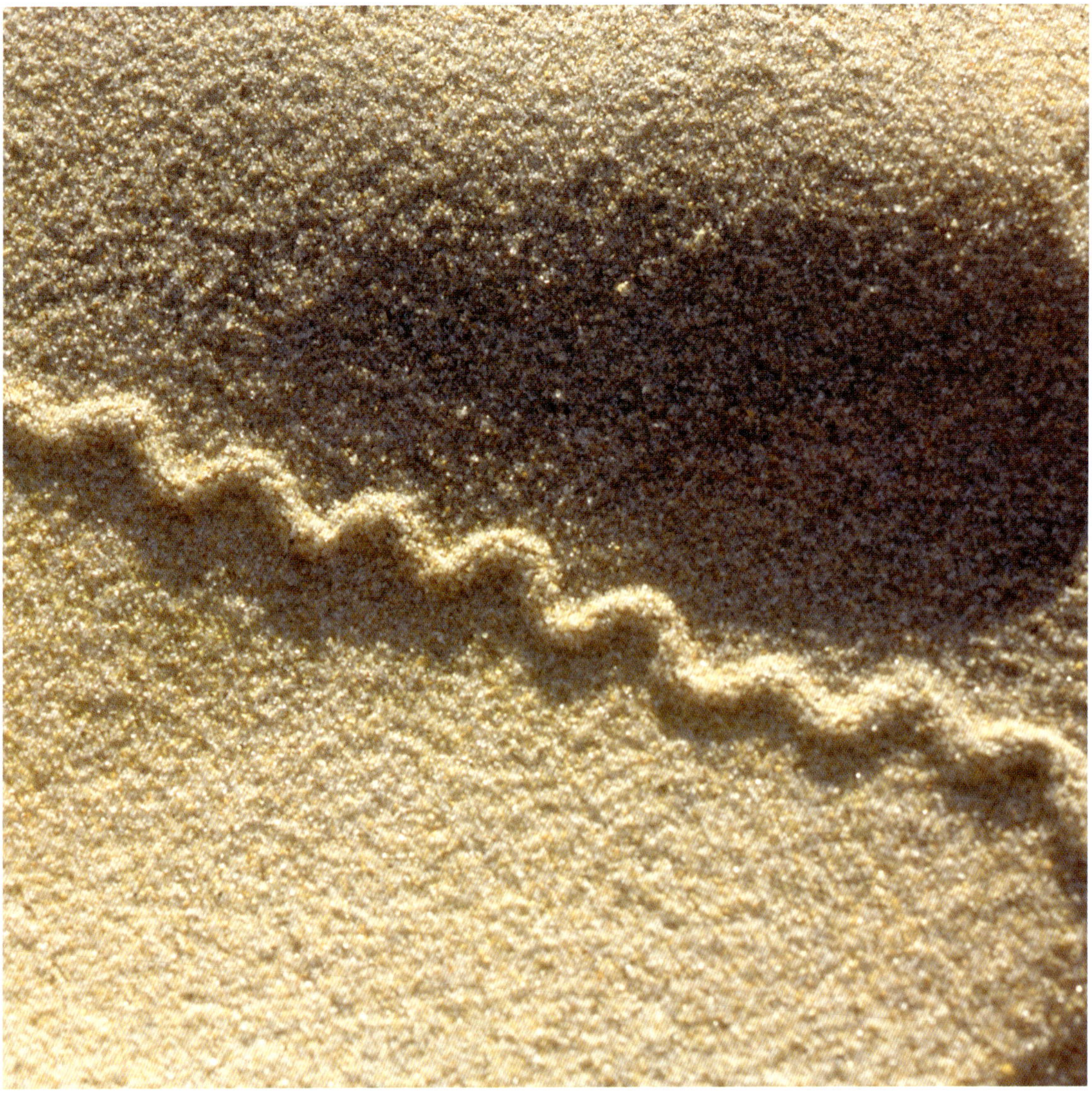

READING THE LAND

"It is so important to read the land, to be observant of the changing colour of the leaves, and the changes in behaviour of the animals, so we become aware and recognise the messages the land is sending us."

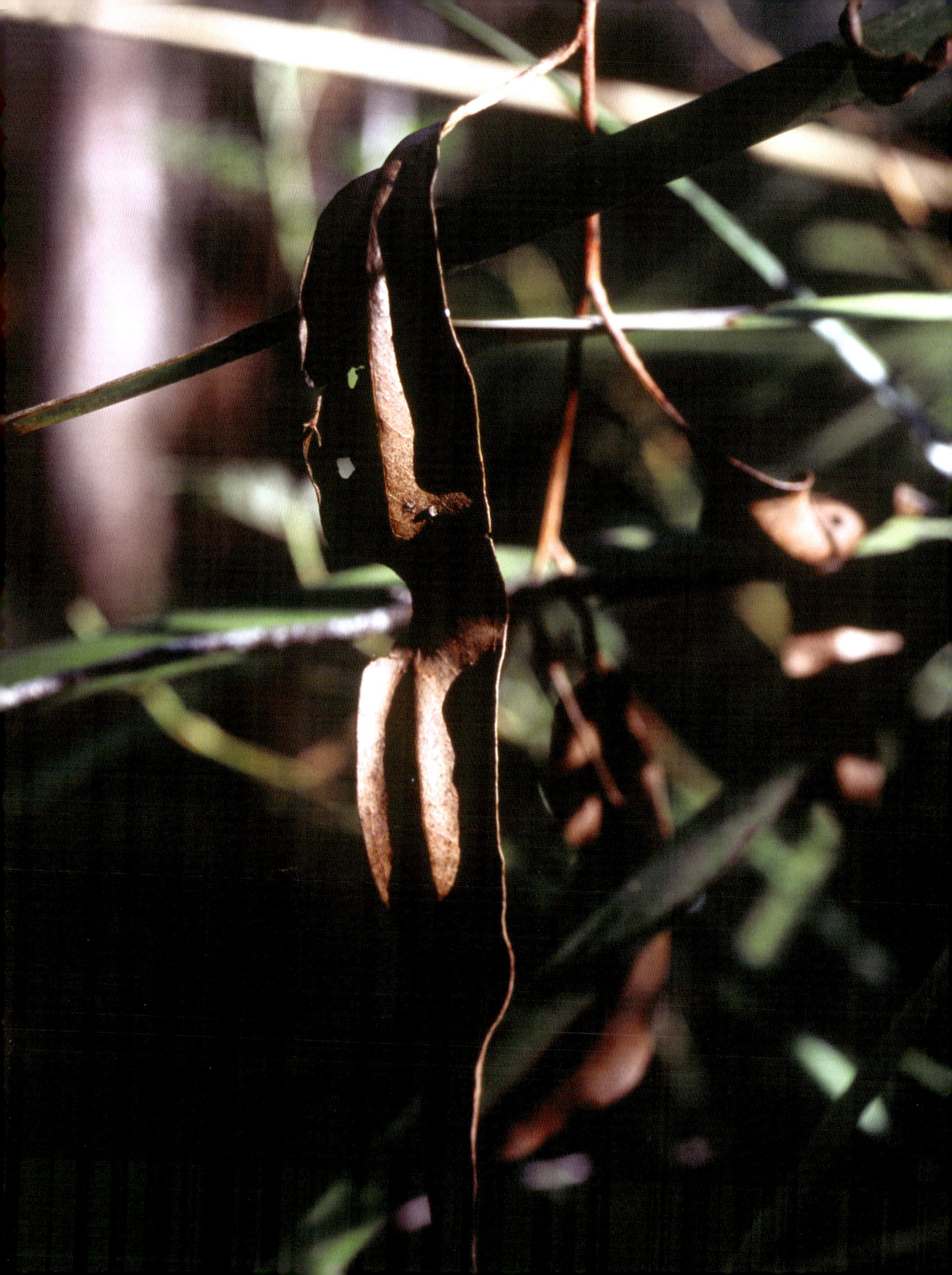

Our people moved around; they were nomadic. They took themseves to other parts of country to follow the seasons and follow the foods. It was a great way to preserve and be with the environment. They travelled from the high country to the forests, to the rivers, to the sea shores. The richness in the variety of foods gave our people health and strength.

We knew what fish would be travelling the coast because of what blossoms we saw and other natural signals that were given on land. We saw the connectedness between the sea and the land. We had our own calendars in nature to let us know the migration of what was in the sea. We could read Grandmother Moon and know when shellfish and other creatures were moving into the shallows to replenish what we had taken from our gathering areas.

From up in the high country there were sources of information, such as the colour of bark on the trees or the colour of the leaves at certain times of a season, that would tell us to venture down the mountains and into the grasslands. Nature has a beautiful way of guiding us and showing us, and explaining to us what was becoming available. We were reading the sacred text of the land.

We travelled slow so we could read the sacred text. Modern time-saving devices just speed up humanity. We are with the land and we read her and take in what she is saying. We realised the enormity of a flower in bloom or a dry leaf or dew on the grasses – the patterns of the earth.

I witnessed my Uncles and father chanting and calling in Koorah Koo-rie wind spirit then getting into the water and slapping the surface of the sea with their sticks. This was a message that went out to the dolphins so they would herd in the fish. The dolphins would drive them into the channels, and we would hunt the fish from there.

These old men were masters of communicating and getting in touch with the spirit of the dolphins. They never went out in a boat and trained the dolphins to do this; they did this through connection of spirit, telepathically. You see, we are creatures of the land, the dolphin from the sea; there is a shared connectedness between us.

It's important for our people to be connected to the past to remember how great we are and can be. These new times are shallow. The power is within us, not in the material objects around us.

Previous page: Animal tracks in the sand.
Left: The changing colour of leaves lets us know when it is time to move from the high country down to the grasslands.

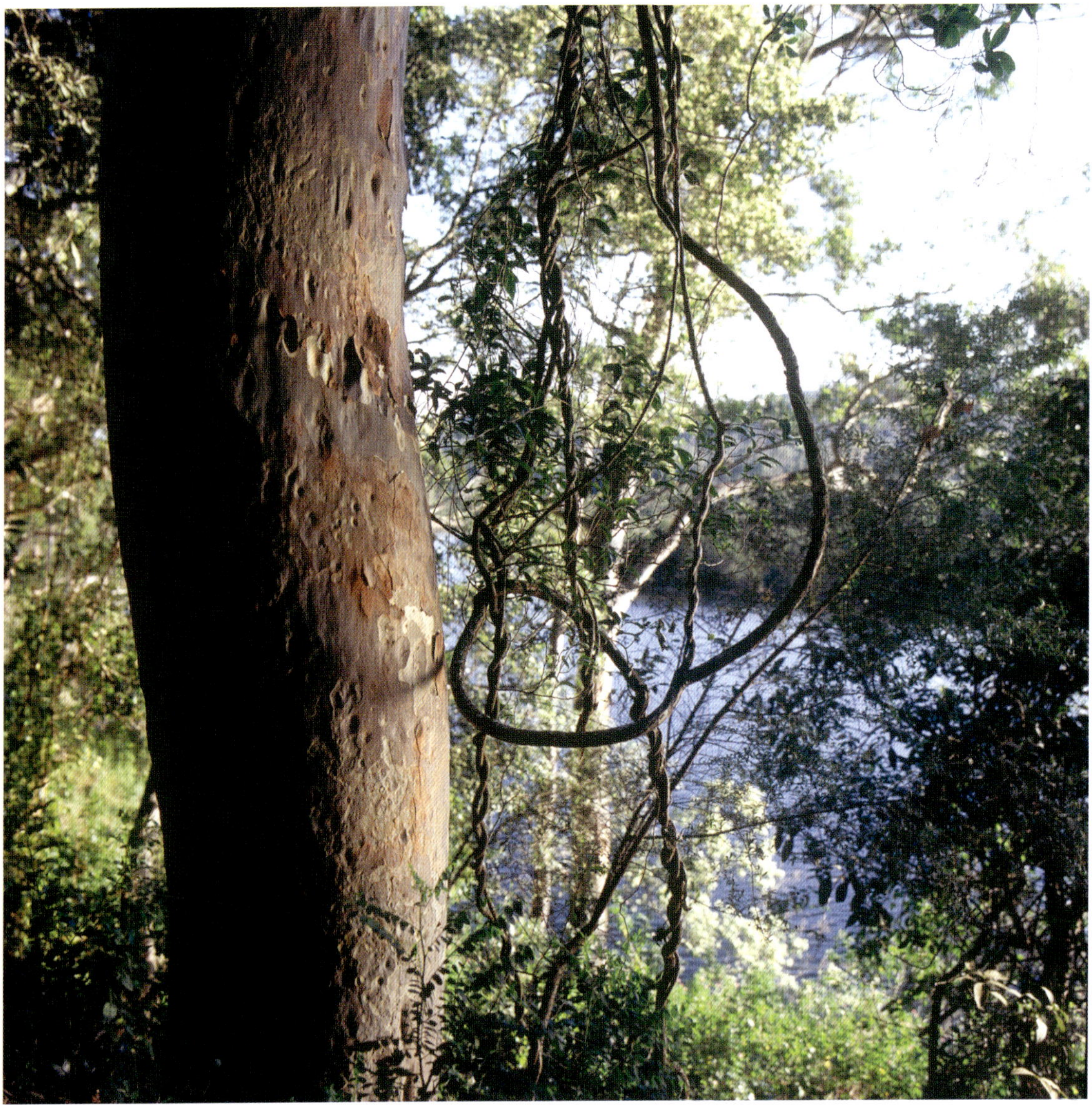

THE SEASONS

"When I take people out into the bush, I ask them to look around and tell me what they see. They look around, but they are not really seeing. They say: 'We just see the bush, Uncle. What do you see?'

'What do I see?' I say. 'I see a supermarket!'"

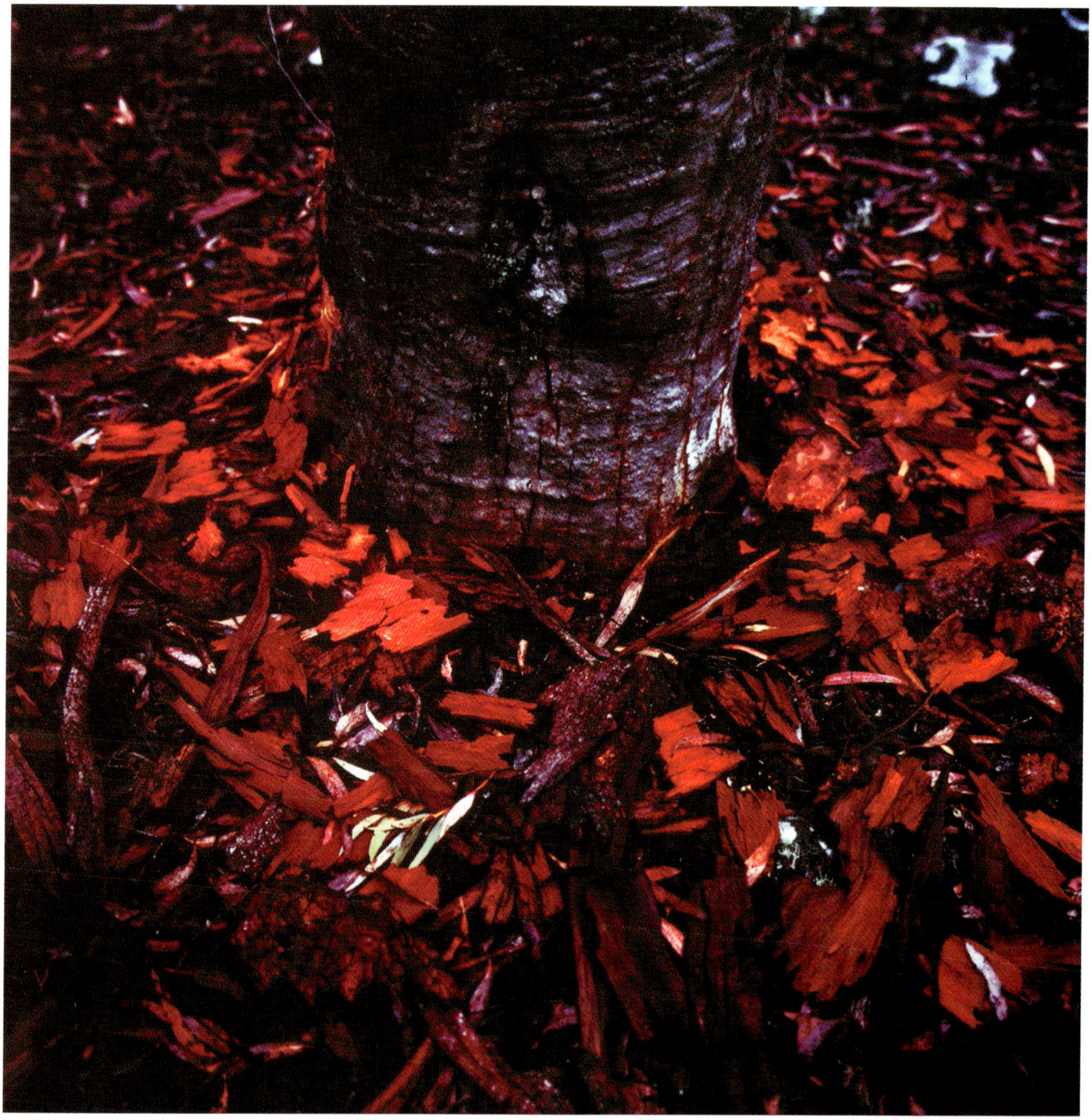

When we look at the seasons changing, drought and flood, we see that what was in balance is out, due to the arrogance of the people of the modern world. Through our greed and selfishness, what was once our need, has now become just our wanting.

We have nine seasons down in Yuin country, and if we look at each of these seasons, we can see what crops are being produced and what is going to be produced. Most of our seasons are indicated by colours: red bark at a certain time of year, yellow blossom, browns and greens. There are nine seasons of Birthing, of signs that tell us to move on and what is maturing.

When we go to take our food from plants or trees, we have to shake that tree three times. If the plant or the trees don't release their crops, then they are not going to give us anything at all. So you can't just stay there and starve and wait until the plant is ready, you must move onto another spot. You see, you have got to remember that trees and plants are also tribal. The tribal plant in one spot can give us this food but we don't want to eat it out. We've also got to leave something for the next mob who come along.

Now we have got to look at the landscape and see we must go to another spot, so we can get food there. Then we might have a bonus. There could be other stuff there. And then when we've finished there, we move on to another spot, and so on.

We are not following the sun, we are following the crops. Following the cupboards or the aisles of what I call the ancient supermarkets of the bush. When we take those fruits that are not ready, that's because of our greed and selfishness, and we are not concerned about the next mob that's going to come behind us. That's what our needs are, our needs are becoming our wanting now.

The red colour of this tree tells us what season we are in. The bark has exploded off and reveals sap, which may be useful to us, help with our healing or be used in some medicine. We can read the colours of nature to see what is good to eat now and what should be left until another time.

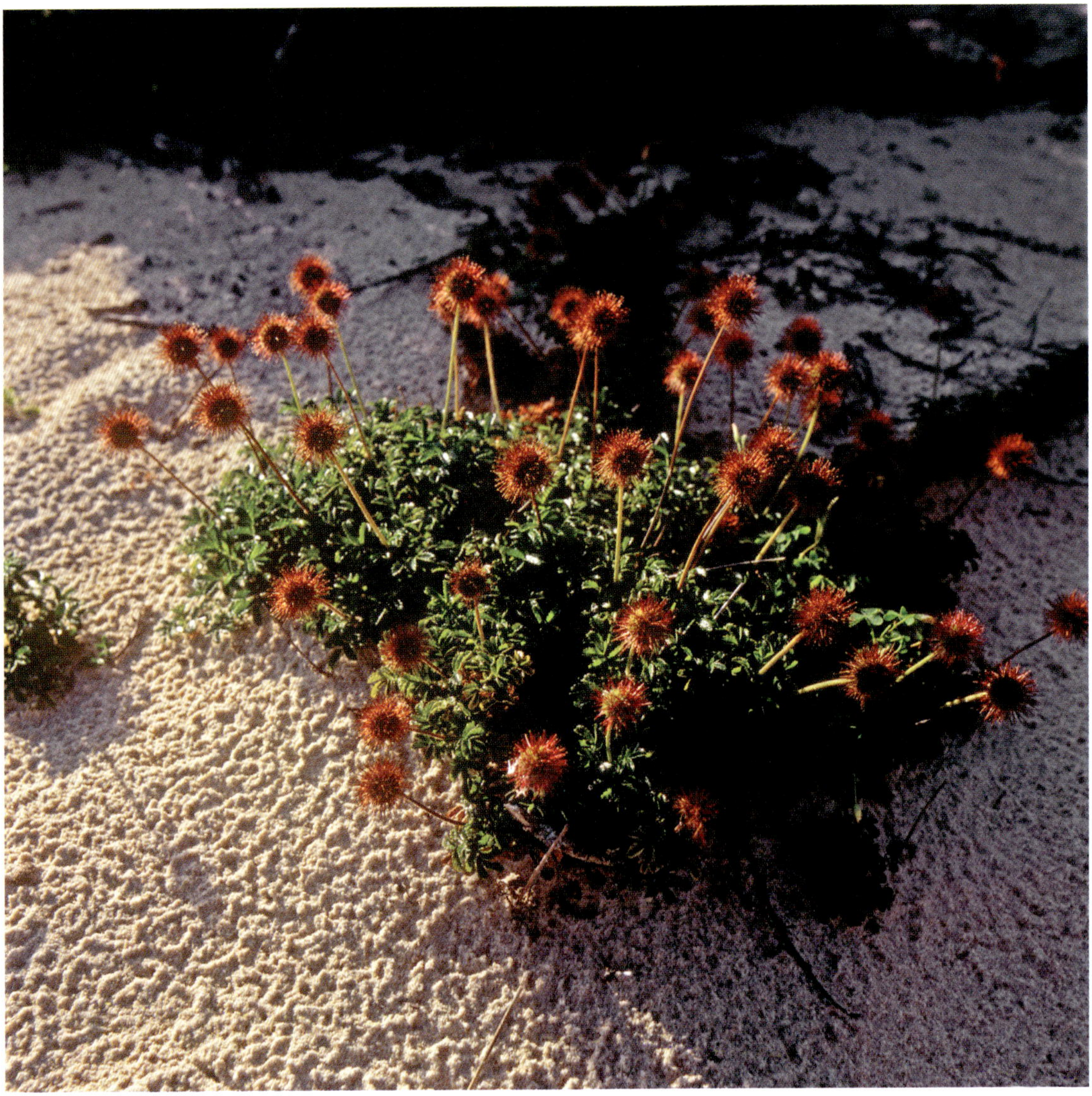

THE THREE PRINCIPLES OF LEARNING

"The three principles of learning are watching, listening and seeing. If we don't follow these principles then we don't learn anything."

I am one of 14 children. Every one of my brothers and sisters was born on the land.

As I was growing up, my teachers were my Uncles. There were five who taught me the way, and my Grandfather Muns was one of my principle teachers. He was so important to my teaching because he was an initiated man. He was a very clever old man with his hands; he was a healer. He taught me about our laws, initiation and healing.

Grandfather Muns comes from the tribe that's down on the Snowy River. Grandfather Muns is the son of a survivor, Charlie Hammond. Charlie was one of the survivors of a massacre at a place called Brodribb River, one of the rivers down near Orbost and Marlo.

Grandfather Charlie was taken and adopted by a white family called Hammond. They gave him the name Charles. That's how he became Charles Hammond. Then Great-grandfather Charlie took a wife and had a son, James. That's why Grandfather Muns was known as James Hammond or Muns Hammond. Muns was his tribal name.

Muns was taken through initiation by some of the principal tribal people within the Gunai people, Kurnai Gunai. The Gunai people were from down around Omeo and towards Delegate on the fringes of the Snowy Mountains. Because I was a descendant of the more southern end of the Yuin people, Grandfather Muns took hold of me and decided to teach me.

Traditional spear making with echidna quills. This was usually done in camp. The quills used were remnants from a feast. The quills were dipped in a poison from a plant and stuck into the side of the spear. You didn't throw these spears; they were used if you got into battle. Anybody with those poisoned quills inside them, well, they were in trouble. They were also handy if you missed a big roo with your hunting spear and he came at you punching and kicking. You could get in quick with the poisoned spear.

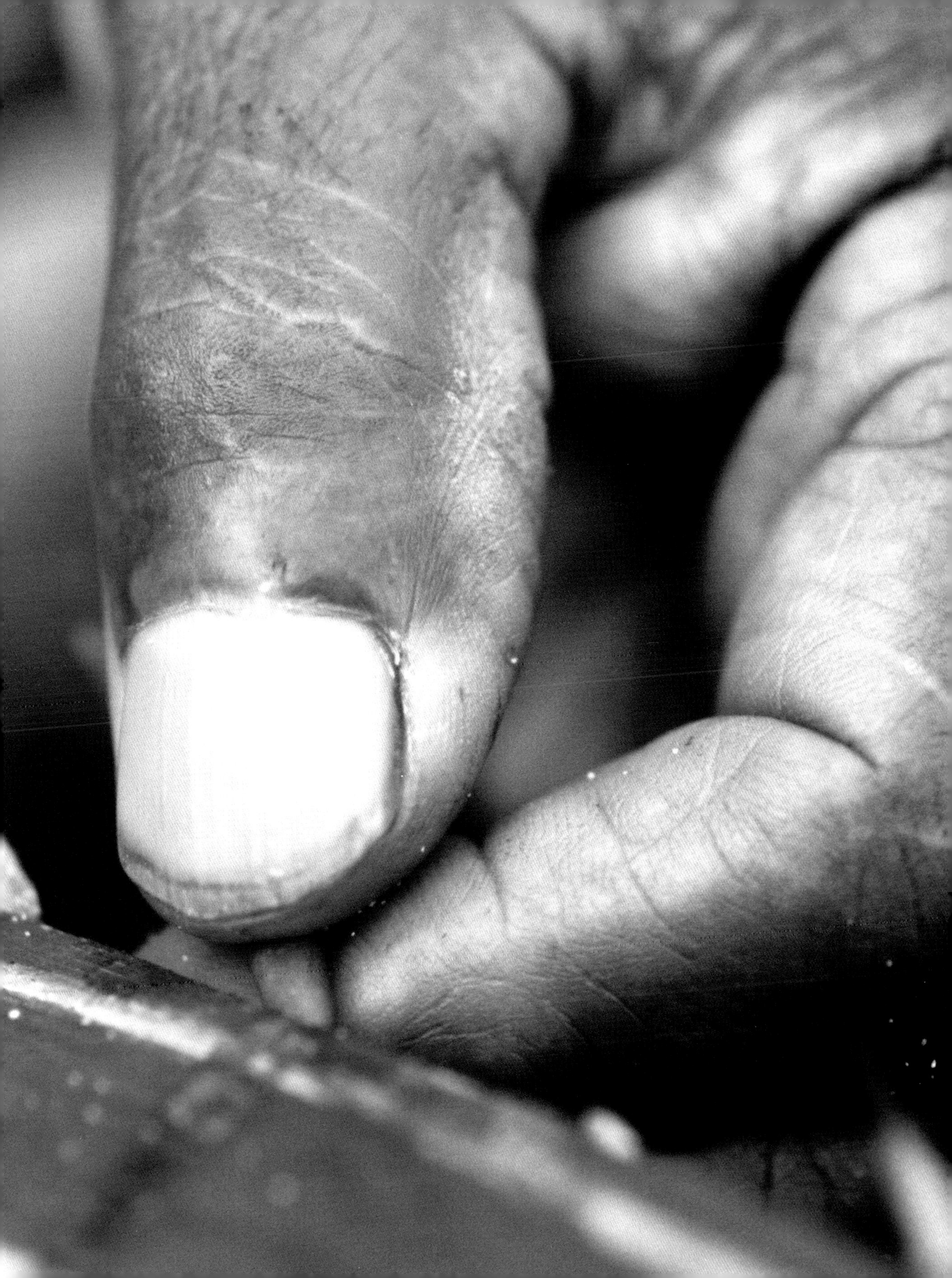

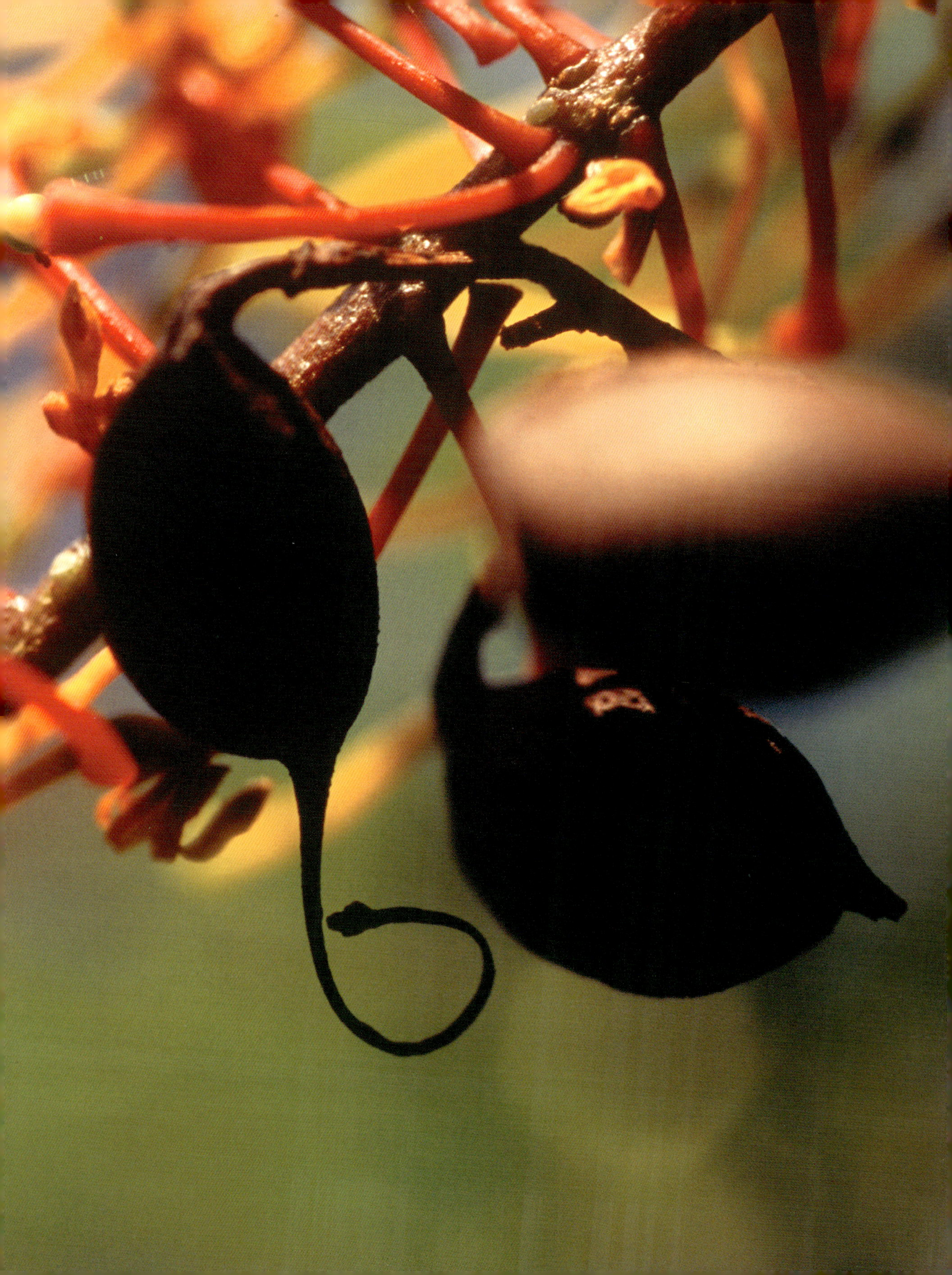

Grandfather Muns taught me all about healing. I was just 10 or 11 when he worked on my appendix. He fixed the problem there; he took out what was wrong. I got up straight away; it was instant. He didn't use a knife; he used psychic healing. Sometimes the healers wouldn't even touch you, just move their hands over the area needing to be healed. But first they would hold or rub their belly just under the naval to access their healing powers. Then those hands would come your way and pull out the sickness, wrapping it around their hands like a ball of wool – you couldn't see it but you could feel it. They would dig a hole and put that sickness in there. In those days there were no modern medicines for our people's sickness so we took care of it ourselves, and some of us still do.

But the first things Grandfather Muns taught me were respect and patience and tolerance. If I had failed with those three simple teachings, then he would never have taken me through the rest, because they were the basics of all the teaching. If I didn't have patience, if I didn't have tolerance and, most of all, if I didn't have respect then he would never have got the other four Uncles to take me through our laws.

Most of the lessons were taught through observation. For example, one day, one of the old Uncles called me when I was walking back to our little humpy, and said to me, 'Come on, Dulumunmun, you have got to go to school.' Of course, Dulumunmun is my tribal name. I went down to the bush and there were four other old men waiting. I am not allowed to use their names, but I can use my Grandfather's because that is permissible. So one of the other Uncles then said: 'Sit down under the tree.'

Healing fruits and berries. With these berries you may notice the colours are also the colours of the Aboriginal flag. The colours are important to notice because if you wanted to use a plant for healing it needs to show particular colours on it otherwise it might be pretty toxic. The colours change according to the season, so you also need to know the right time to use a plant for healing. If you don't you might get ill and kick the bucket.

So I sat down under the tree and I just waited, and I waited and then I thought, 'Well, they are just standing over there talking.' So I decided to occupy myself and I grabbed a little stick and I started playing with it in the dirt, you know? Scratching some patterns. Then one of the old guys looked around and said to me, 'We never told you to do that. We never told you to pick up a stick.' That's all he said, but the command in his voice was such an authority to me that I knew that the only thing to do was to sit. And so I threw the stick away and that was it. I just sat.

Then they turned around a couple of hours later and one of them said, 'Now Dulumunmun, you can go now. You have learned enough for today.' And I jumped up and I dusted off my pants and I walked up the hill, and I thought: 'Well, what did I learn? What did I learn?' Then I realised that I learned patience and tolerance and respect from when I didn't challenge them about playing with the stick, you know? So, I felt good about myself. I didn't have to be told two or three times, and I guess that's what they looked for in a young student.

A lot of the lessons were similar to that. They were all about observation. Observation and just using eyes is one of the methods of survival. If people didn't observe and look around and notice how and when different colours come to the different plants, they never would have known what was growing next, when their next foods were coming, or how far away or how close they were and all that kind of thing. So observation is about 50 000 years of what I call legacies, handed down from generation to generation. Learning to obey was a great principle of the respect Law that was instilled in me.

The fern frond represents young life and can also be used as antiseptic... we call it bush antiseptic. If you have a little cut you take a little bit of the plant and dab it on the cut. You don't need to take the whole leaf and squash it. Leave some for it to regrow.

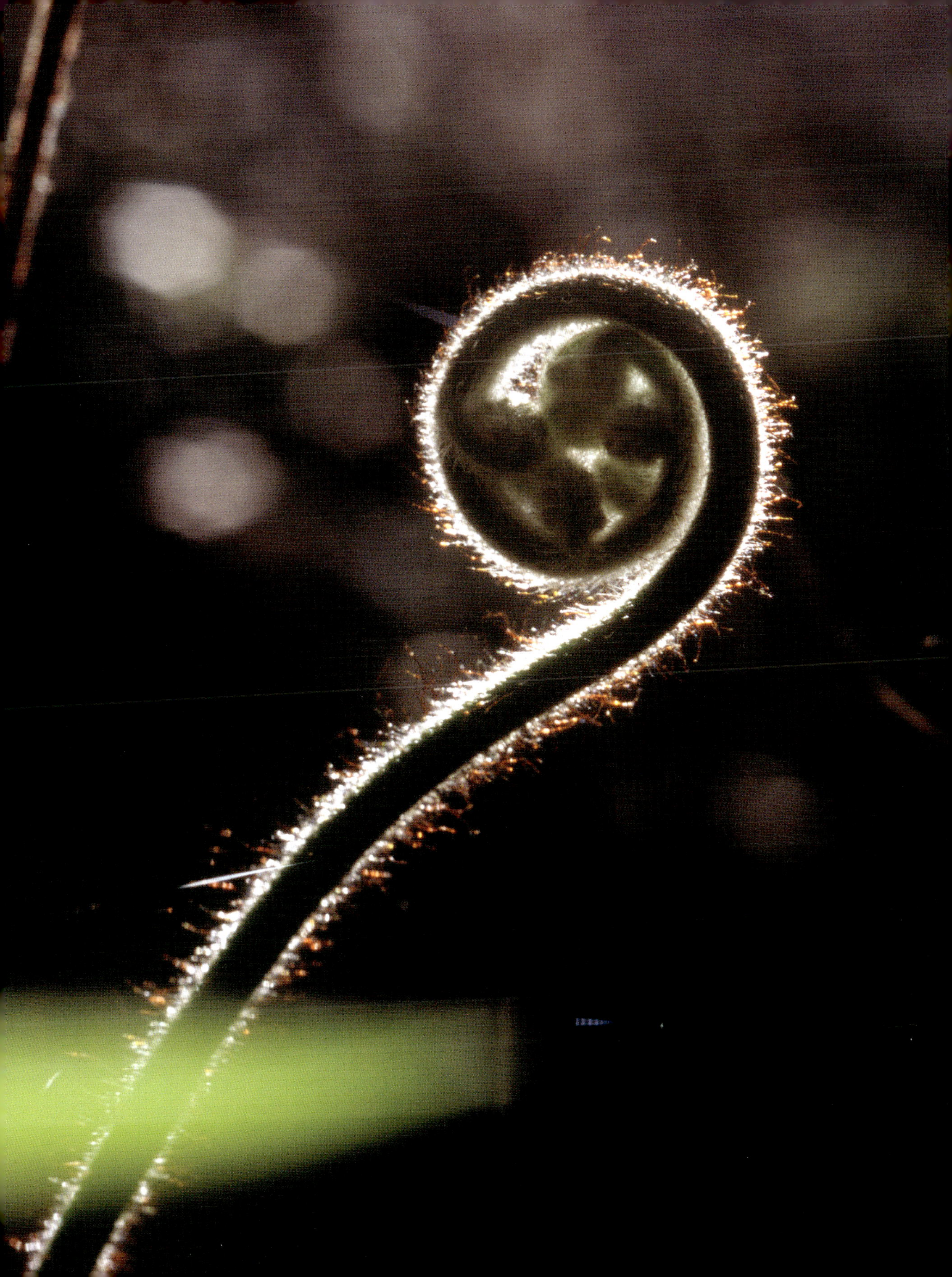

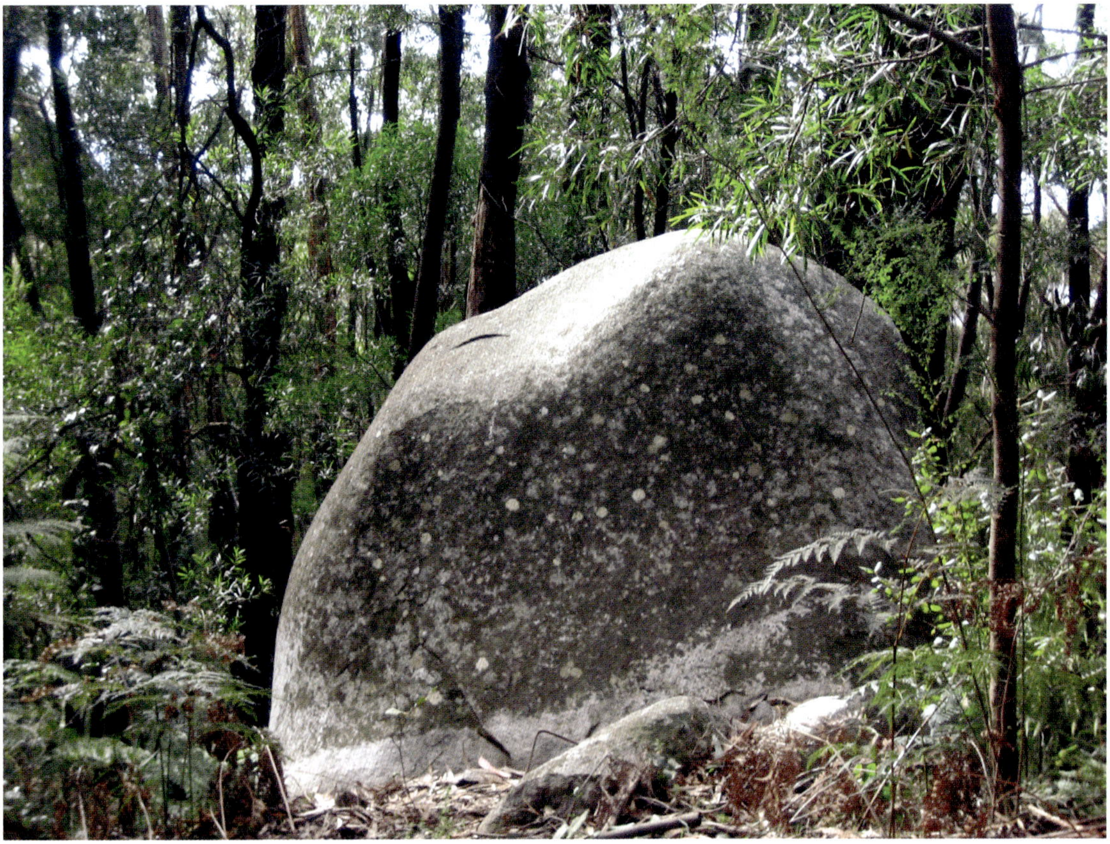

THE TRUTH OF TRADITIONAL KNOWLEDGE

"The two lads in the water on the next page are my grandkids. They are in the river so they feel the cold. See, that's a pretty cold river. But the other thing I got them to feel was an understanding of the power of the water and the cleansing of the water and what it was doing for their bodies.

When they got into that cold water, I told them, 'Now you stay there until you're a little bit colder and then when you come out your body temperature will just shoot up.' They said, 'Pop, we'll freeze to death!' and I said, 'No you won't, you'll learn a little bit of truth about going from freezing to warmth, and you must believe me on that because that's the truth of the knowledge that my grandfather and Uncles have passed onto me.'"

Grandfather Sun is such a powerful being. Scientists see Grandfather Sun as a planet, so many miles or kilometres away, but Grandfather is here on earth, everywhere, in every bit of coal and wood. I can hold him in my hand and build a fire with him and be close to him. He will put heat on your back when you get out of a cool mountain stream and warm you up. To get away from him you have to enter the water or step into the shade. He gives us light and warmth. But how far away is he, really? We are more connected than we really know: and yet distance and time alter thought and distort the truth.

We already know that we are connected to nature. We already know that we should be in touch with it. And a lot of our mob now are getting more connected because of a growing awareness that is happening about their homelands, about their genealogies. Also, traditional knowledge and language is now being more spoken about more openly. Our people are wanting to know and when they start asking, well, then the genes inside them click on and, because it's in their bloodline and running through their genealogy, they are getting more connected to the old ways.

But what's coming into the teachings now, is different. It's a different lot of teachings now with our mob, even to what there was in the early settlers' time. So distance and time before the settlers came is different to distance and time after they came because they altered a lot of our truth. We were being told we were this and that, and in particular, we were told we were half-caste, or quarter-caste, one eighth and all the different castes, which is all bull. I can't understand that, you see. I am being looked on as some sort of measuring implement, yet I hold knowledge, I hold knowledge of thousands of years of Dreaming, and my blood is running full of traditional knowledge. So I won't let what people tell me and put into me distort me. We have got to keep the purities of traditional knowledge there. Distance and time alter thoughts and distort the truth.

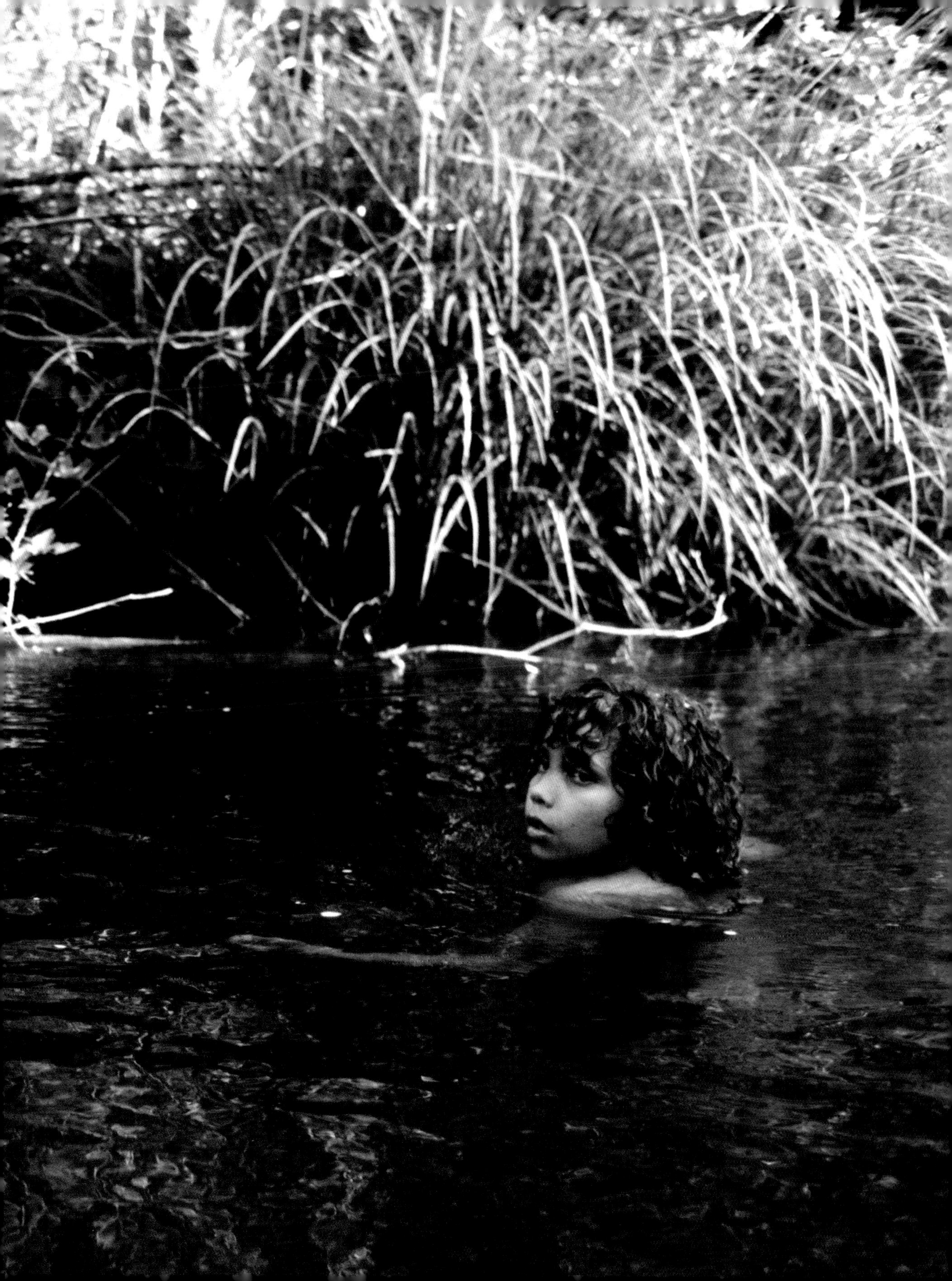

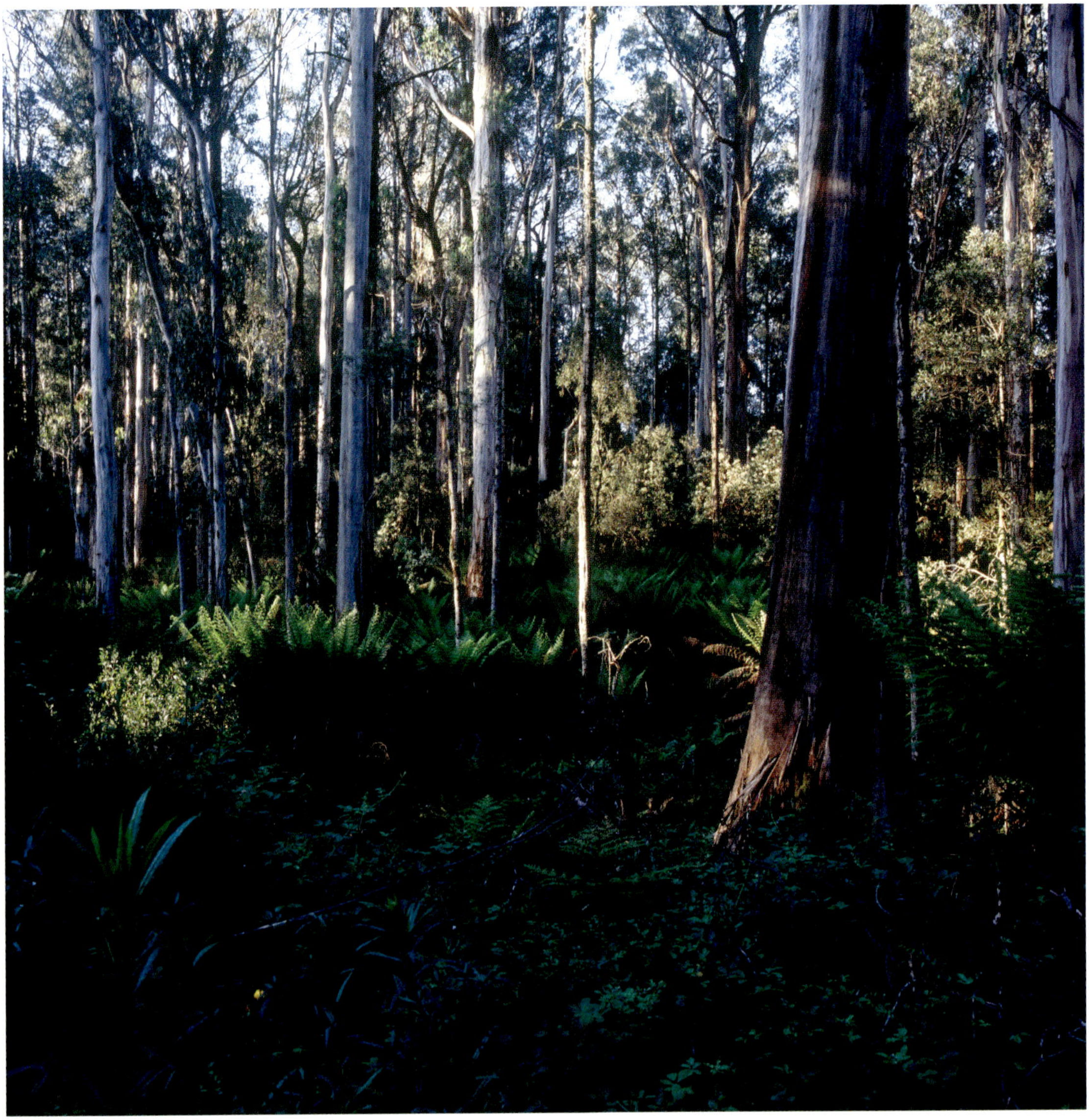

MY TEACHERS

"*Our way of life, our tribal life, our community life, was based on a series of teachings and each related to one or the other for a specific reason, such as safety, health, medicines or observing sacred spots.*"

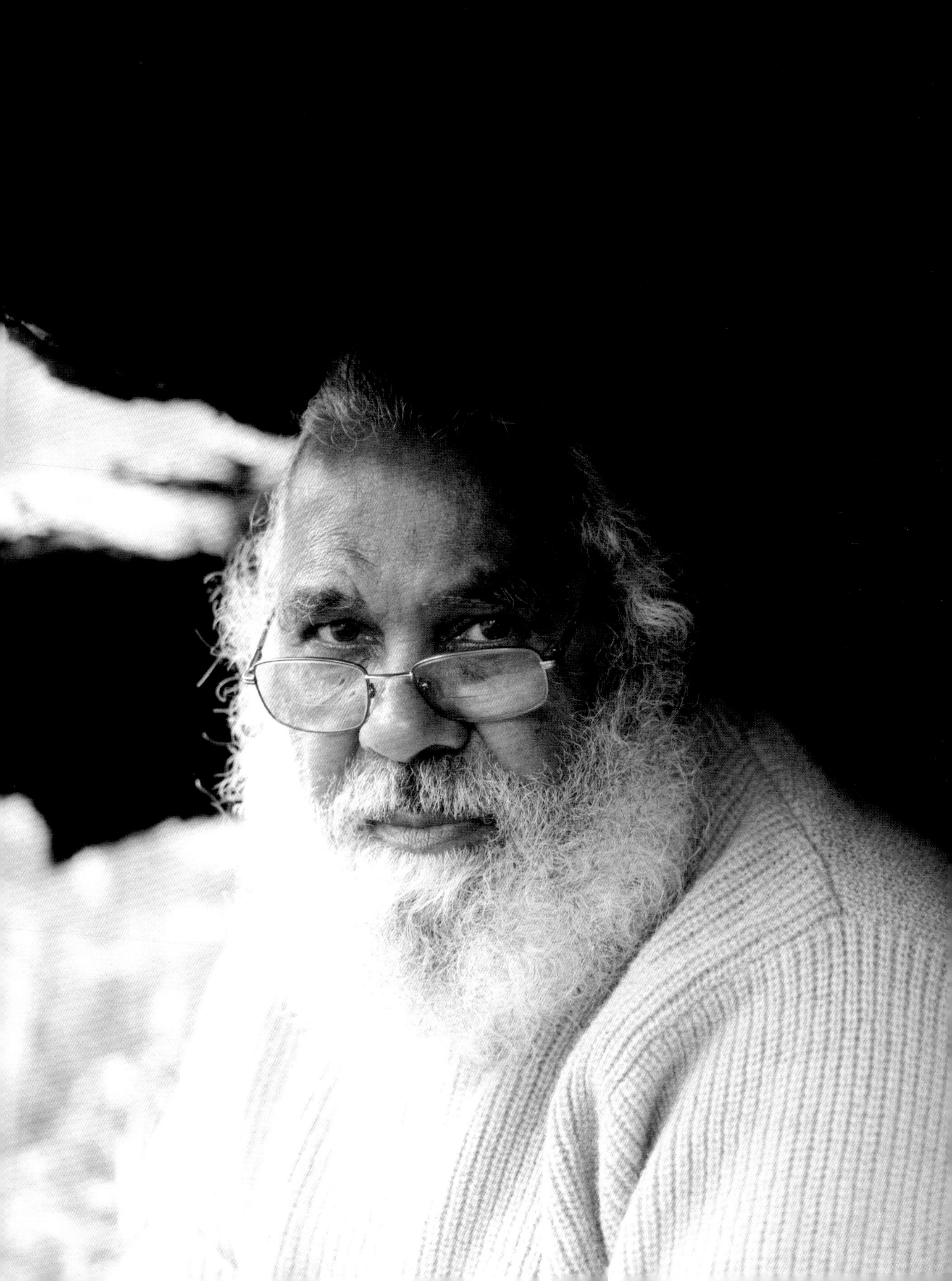

I've taken many men through the Law of the land, the Law of respect. What I teach the young ones is never ask 'Why?'. When you have been told something within law you do not question it. You hold it in sacredness.

Young men are taught different aspects of law to suit who they are, and that becomes their law to hold. Even their chores are different. One may be in charge of the fire, to make it and maintain it, so he's taught where the fire belongs and which way Koorah Koo-rie wind spirit will come and affect the fire. Some young men may be taught other aspects so they can back each other up and step in and support each other. All those young men hold a piece of the jigsaw that fits in with the others. Put all this together and there's a functioning community right there.

My five Uncles and my grandfather were my teachers but they were more than teachers; they were masters of law and healing. They taught me continuously for 17 years. I was taught alone. They would take me out bush at certain times. Sometimes it would be ten days at a time. Ten days of silence in the bush was one lesson. They took me away to learn communication without sound.

This was pretty trying for me. There was no talking, not even by those five old Uncles. I couldn't ask them a question like, 'What can I do to help around the camp?' All I had to do was use observation methods and just notice what one fella was doing, building up a shelter, another fella probably getting water, another fella getting food prepared and so on like that. Then I had to piece it together that each one of these old men was doing something, so what am I going to do? I saw one old fella preparing the food and I thought, 'Well, how is he going to cook? Oh, I suppose I probably should go and get the wood for the fire.' And that became my law at that time, to go and get wood. It was obvious that something had to be done, so I went and gathered the wood. I threw all the wood in one big pile and I was so pleased with myself that I had done this job, and I just sort of sat back and looked at my great work. Then one old fella walked past the wood I had piled in a heap and he grabbed a piece and took it over a bit further and dumped it.

Part of my teachings came from lots of my uncles and aunties. If we wanted to go from point A to point B and we asked Mum or Dad if we could go they would say to us, 'Go and ask Aunty so and so and Uncle so and so.' So we would go and ask the aunty and uncle and they would say, 'Well, you'd better go and ask that uncle and aunty over there,' so then we would go over to the others and so on like that. We would be saying things like 'But we've already asked Mum and Dad!' and be whingeing a bit. Finally we'd go to another aunty and uncle and they would say 'Okay, you can go over there but you've got to go that way.' What we didn't realise was that by having to ask everyone's permission we were letting the whole community know where we were. The last lot of uncles and aunties we asked would know where other kids or people were and would direct us to the safety of them. So all the teachings of my uncles and aunts were important to my safety.

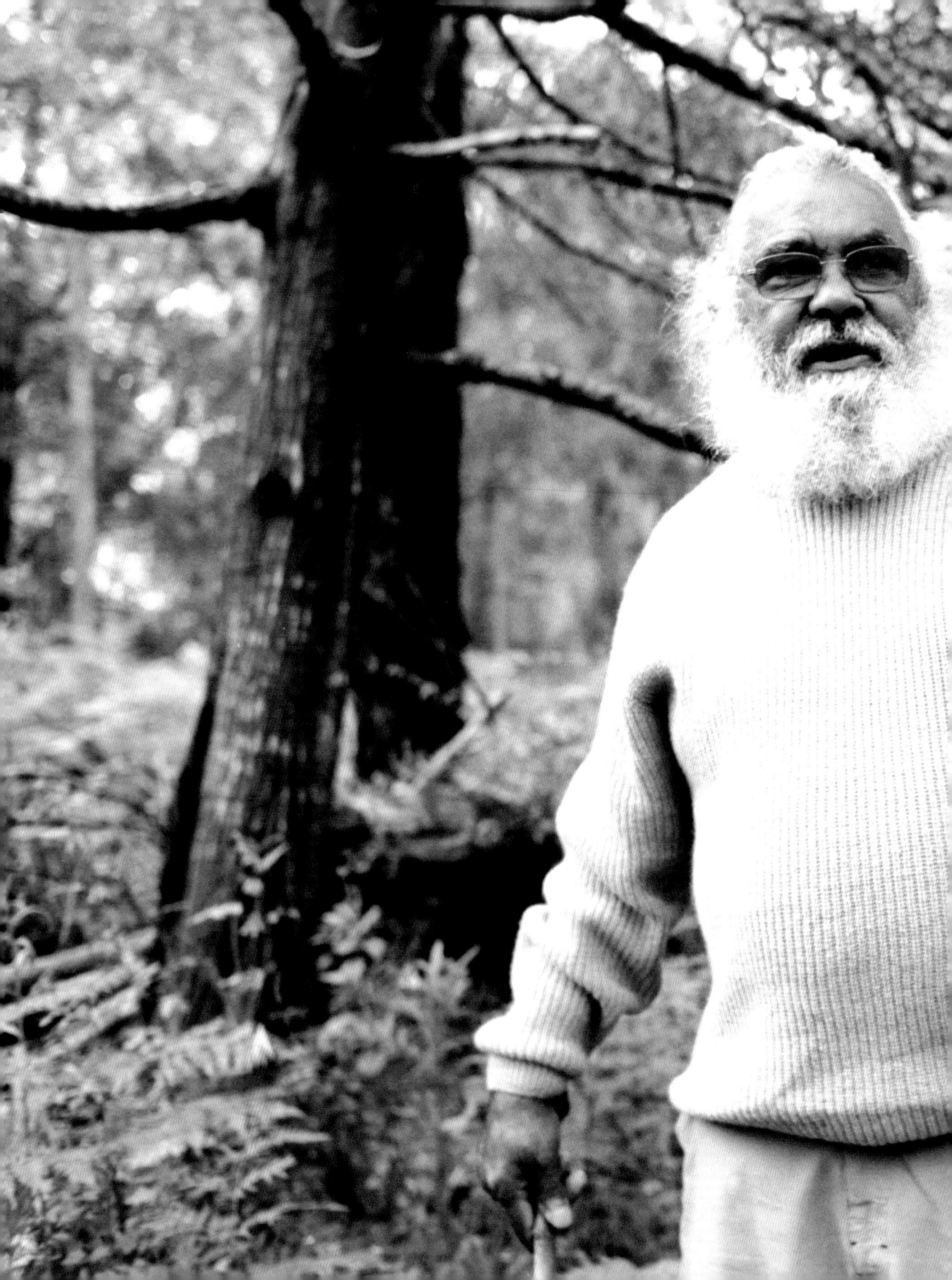

'Nothing wrong with that log,' I thought. Then he went and did something else, and when he came back he picked up another piece of wood and he took it over and dumped it over where this other one was. I thought, 'Oh yes, we have got to have two fires, one for cooking on and one for ceremony. I have got to get enough wood for two fires.' So when I thought my job was finished, off I go again and get more wood for the ceremonial fire. That was the kind of thing that was taught to me in silence. This was what we would call talking with no voice. It was wonderful to do that communication.

Another lesson my Uncles taught me was about concentration, discipline and respect. We were out in the bush walking along and three Uncles would be in the front and two would be at the back, and one out of the three in front would talk to me, just chatting. The Uncles were using English at times, you know, because bringing in some of the other languages from different parts of the Yuin country would have been so distracting to me.

Then one of the old fellows out at back would become the Devil's advocate and he would stick his head around and look me in the eye and say, 'Did you hear what he said? Are you taking any notice what he's talking about?' And of course I was, but the first time I looked around and I said to that Uncle, 'Yes, yes, I am listening,' and then bang – I copped it right on the head! And it happened about two or three times, and I thought, 'Well, I am not going to get a thick ear out of this every time they talk. So I am making a mistake here somewhere.' Then I realised what it was. I realised that every time that they ducked their face in front of me and started to talk, I would lose concentration on what the three in front was telling me.

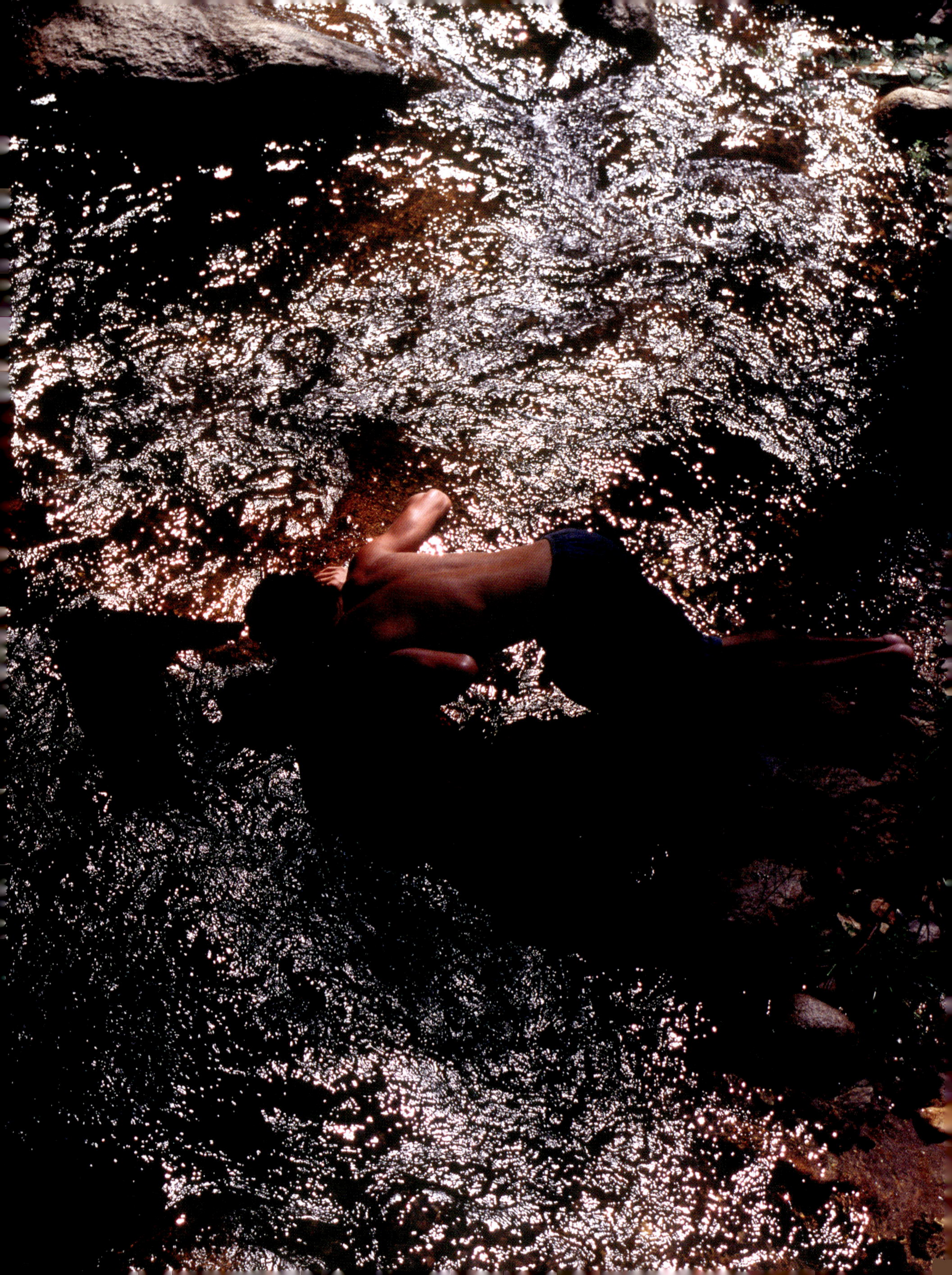

So that taught me to just say nothing and ignore the two Uncles from the back. And I felt pretty miserable about that because every time that they asked me something, it was like they expected an answer, but that wasn't appropriate at that time. They were there just to see if they could distract me from these other three. And if they could distract me from these other three, well, then I was in serious trouble because I might forget what I was being told. So I learned to hold my composure and wait. When an Uncle would stick his beak around and try to ask me these questions, I would let it go. When I didn't answer the two at the back, they would say, 'Oh he's being disrespectful see?' And it was all baiting. I thought 'No, no I am not even going to talk to you,' you know? So I am feeling miserable because I thought I am showing disrespect to my Elders here, because I am not answering. So I am in between being respectful to them and being respectful to the three in front of me. I was wondering, 'Where does my priority lie?'

I was just feeling miserable and guilty. So when the Uncles would switch positions, the ones in front moving to the back, I would just say, 'Well done, Uncle. Sorry, Uncle. Sorry I didn't answer you when you were asking me questions, but I just didn't want to be disrespectful to the three Elders in front of me.' That was the right thing to say. It's all about discipline.

My teaching went on for about 17 years. And when you look at that length of teaching, it's not long at all because your teaching goes on and on. Once you start to look at the landscape and bush and what the land taught you, you realise you are being taught all the time. Nature is the greatest teacher of all.

After the awareness that some of those old guys instilled in me, all I had to do was just keep watching out for different lessons coming through.

They gave me the legacies. From the age of seven up, I have stuck to the legacies taught to me of land management and survival.

Today I don't use a computer but I receive emails from the land; they're spiritual ones. Ten days of silence gave me time to look around and watch the indicators, to observe and study life. It taught discipline and respect. I did have the bush orchestra, the singing of the birds in the morning, the natural world to tune into. This gave me time to listen and accept what I was asked to do; my masters were teaching me to watch the land talk to me. Now, when I go out onto the land, I watch and listen to the world without making a sound – and through this other dimensions open up.

We are never alone out there on the land, our relatives of nature – the trees, grasslands, rocks, animals – they are our family; we treat them respectfully.

My grandson Max drinking from Goongarah River in Victoria. This is my great-grandfather's country.

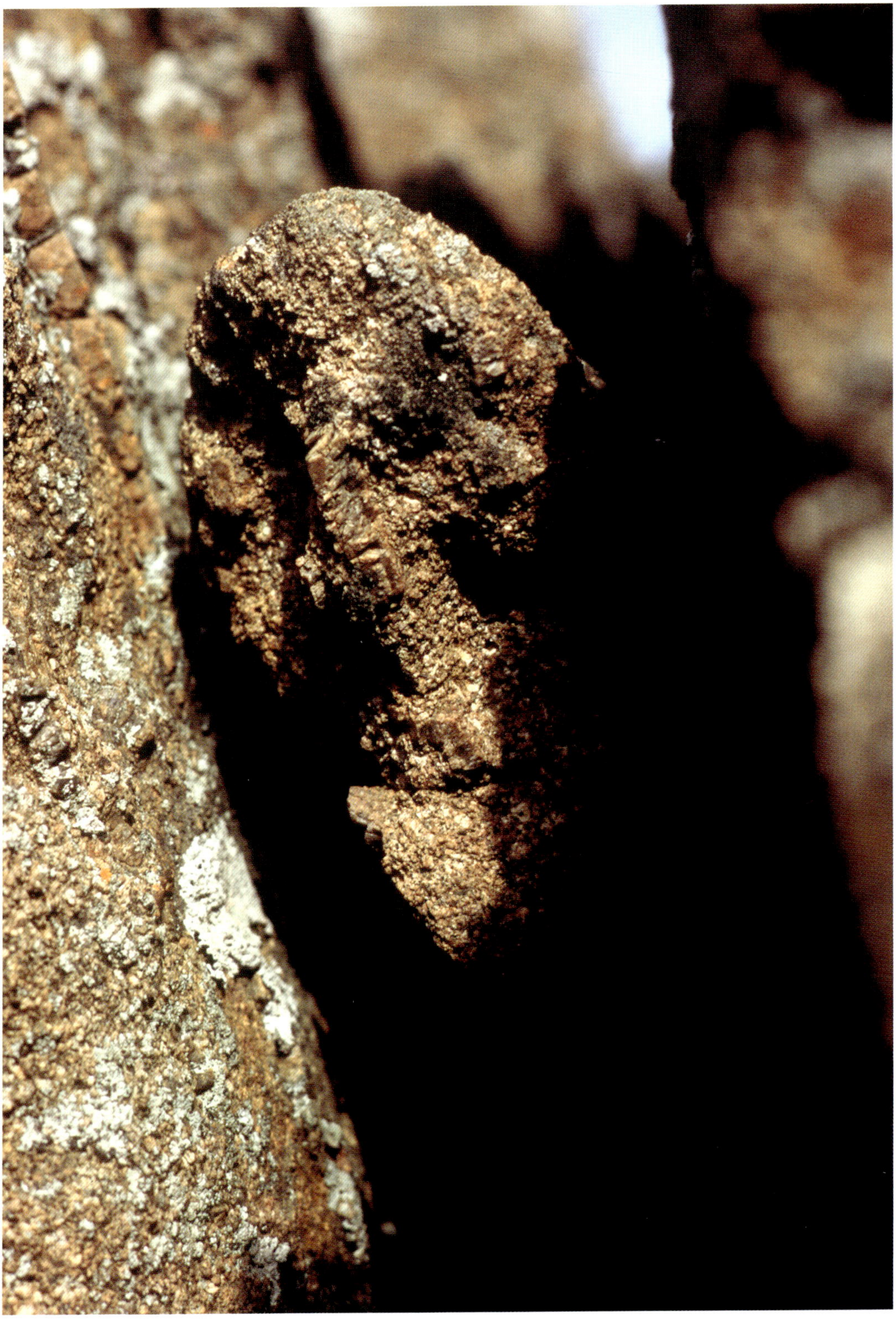

OUR LAWS AND PUNISHMENT

"Our laws are about protection; protection of our safety and protection of Mother Earth. Laws are living things – they are our way of life."

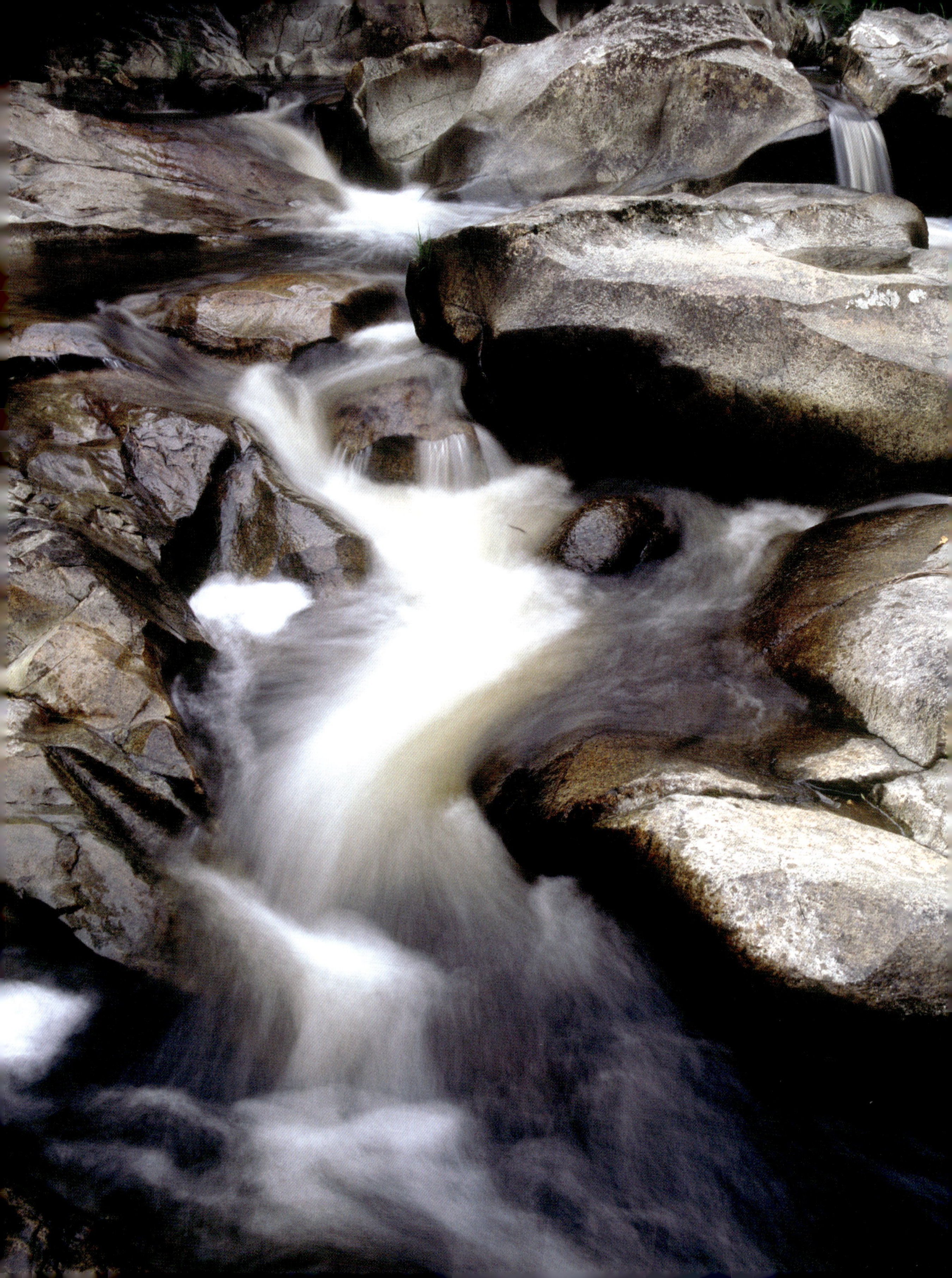

Our laws are about living things and we must obey them. They help us with our morals, our ethics and discipline, and they help us live a natural life, closer to the natural and spiritual world. With our laws the punishment can be severe, very severe – such as being speared in the leg, banished from the community or, to a lesser degree, being made to sit on a stinging nettle. We have the Bugeenj [*Kadaitja or featherfoot*] men. They are trained in killing with spear or club, and they are trained in psychic killing. They can point the bone and kill as punishment.

Once judgement has been passed by the Elders, the punishment is handed down. There are no lawyers in Koori law to bend a lie into a false truth, your own spirit is your witness. Our law is not a written one; it is told and it is to be respected and abided by. The law is not explained in wordy detail; it is enough to be told 'Don't go there.' Holding law needs no explanation, only the respect of holding it, keeping it. Just like when I was told to it sit down – not pick up a stick and start drawing, but just to sit down.

If you broke a law then you got punished. But punishment isn't always about getting whacked with a stick by an Uncle. Sometimes the damage you did to yourself when you broke a law was punishment enough. Look at the rocks in this photo. If you wanted to look for yabbies near these rocks you needed to look at the swiftness of the water and realise that the rocks are slippery. An Uncle might say, 'Be careful where you tread,' but nothing about the slipperiness of the rocks. If you didn't obey the Uncle and look to what the water was telling you, then you would slip because you didn't hold your Law of respect for the Uncle, the water and the rocks. Sometimes if you questioned an Elder, you would be punished by not being told a valuable piece of information about a plant or an animal, because you had shown you were not ready to learn about it yet. That would be another form of punishment.

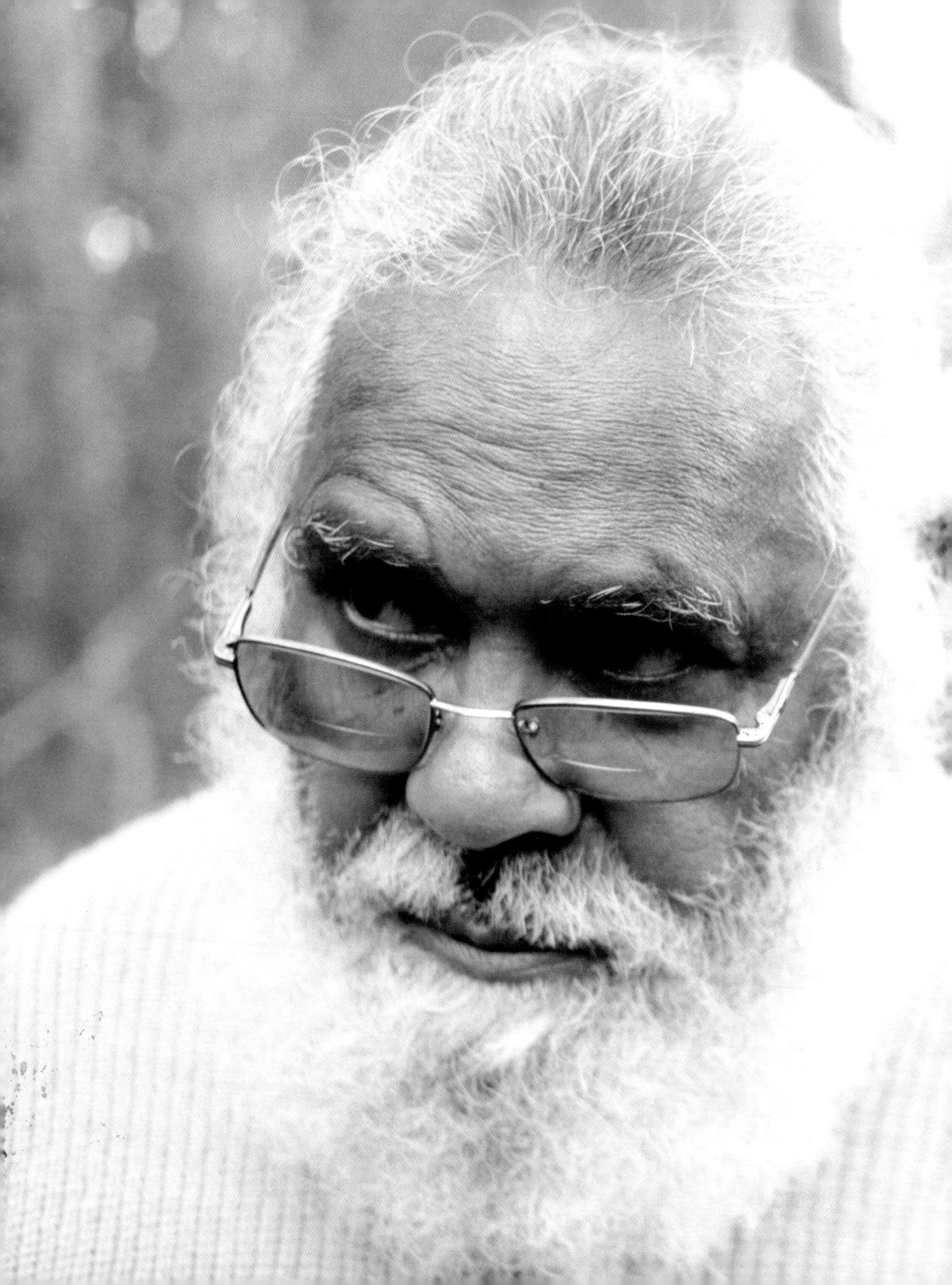

You should never question the Elders. When you ask 'why?' or 'what for?' you are disrespecting your Elders' order and you are being very disrespectful. So you never do that. If you go over into an area where you have been told not to go, well, then you are likely to get whacked. If you are a grown man you are likely to get speared. You are not told why you should not go into an area but you should think that an area might be sacred. It's important that you obey without question, and you do it even today. Everyone does it in modern times today. Especially if you are driving a car you obey the colours of the traffic lights, red, amber and green. If you go through that red one you break a law and you get a fine. You get hit in the pocket. It doesn't hit your leg or your head – it hits the pocket. In today's society, hitting the pocket is hitting your survival.

So when those old people said, 'You don't go over to that waterhole,' you don't go near that waterhole. That waterhole could be a sacred waterhole. That tree could be a sacred tree. That rock could be a sacred rock. Those places of sacredness you stay out of without question. So you are then holding your Law of discipline. You are holding your Law that has been handed down to you just by that order of, 'Don't go there.' You are putting that into practice. Aboriginal culture is living law. All cultures are living law; we just don't often look at it that way in modern times.

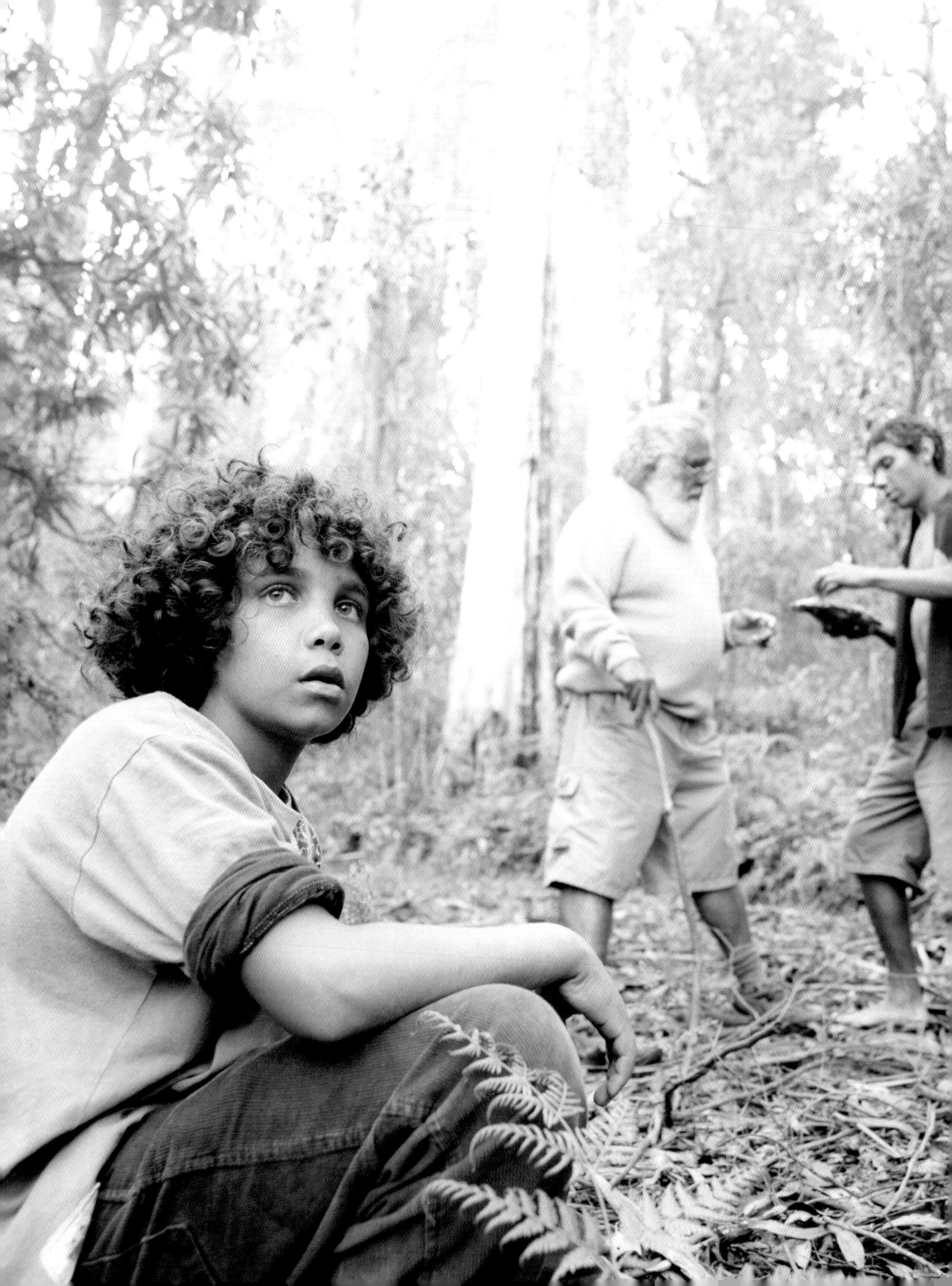

I've used the Laws of respect we hold for women with the young men that have battered their spouses and are about to go to jail. I take them out onto the land and tell them the story about Ngardi and about respecting the land, about respecting Mother Earth.

And they often say to me, 'Yeah, well, Mother Earth is important to me.' And then I will say to them: 'Well go and dig a hole over there.' And some of these young men look at me with blank faces and say, 'Uncle Max, we're not being disrespectful to you here, but you're telling us to go and dig a hole in the Mother,' and ask for what purpose.

And that's when I know that I have them, and then I say to them, 'Okay, so you wouldn't go and dig a hole in a bit of dirt over there, in that bit of the land, but you can batter your woman, your flesh woman, who is bearing your children, and you can batter her and bruise her and have no respect for her.' And the penny drops. Then they start to understand the respect Law. It becomes a very valid point of that part of their creation story.

Teaching Kyandle and Max III down in great-grandfather's country, Goongarah, Victoria.

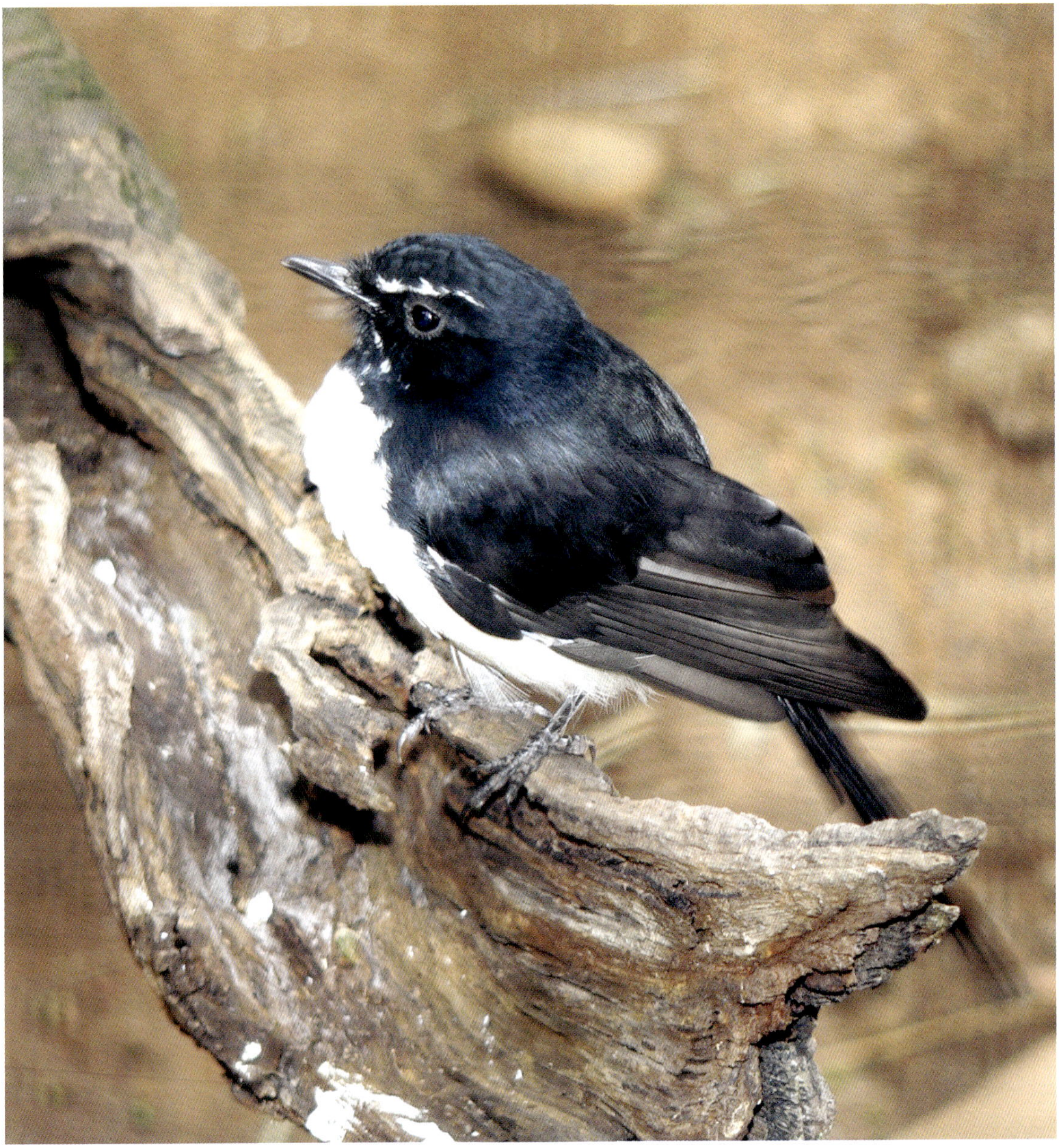

TOTEMS

"Each mob has a collection of totems that represent special areas or animals to their community. It's a way of preserving the ecology. Mobs can't or won't eat those particular totems because if they ate everything they found there would be nothing left for other mobs to eat. As an extra protection, each person within the mob has their own personal totem as well. If I ate one of my grandkids' personal totems I could be in big trouble."

My nation's totem is the black duck (umbarra) and my family totem is the Willie Wagtail. My personal totem is the plover. A totem is whatever comes near you when you are born. Your mother, father or Uncles don't decide. It is whatever comes near you. When I was born, people said, 'Look here, hey, have a look here, this little fella just flew in here and that little fella is just born.' So I was told I must look after that totem, the plover, because that little fella came in and looked after me when I was first born, when I was on my first breath of air.

You must protect your totem at all times. When I see a plover I give it a lot of respect. I want to watch for his little nest in the sand, and I have got to make sure that I tell people he is there, instead of throwing sticks and stuff at him. I have got to tell them: 'Hey don't do that. He's got family here, and they are laying in the sand somewhere.' I say, 'We are protecting his birthright; he's protecting his family. So just leave him alone.' So that's my right, to protect that aggressive little plover when he's nesting.

Our laws apply to our totems. We don't eat our totems; they are held in high regard and respected. The whole of the Yuin Nation, from the Snowy River up to the escarpment of Wollongong, all of our people don't eat umbarra, one of our most significant totems. Umbarra is our friend. However, an outsider with permission may come into our country and eat umbarra.

Everything we take from the land and sea – plants, berries, animals, fish – we ask these things permission or thank them as they are giving up their life for us to eat. This is another respect Law, asking for permission to eat is the right thing to do as we are being given a gift that nourishes us. We must always practise the Laws of respect in everything we do.

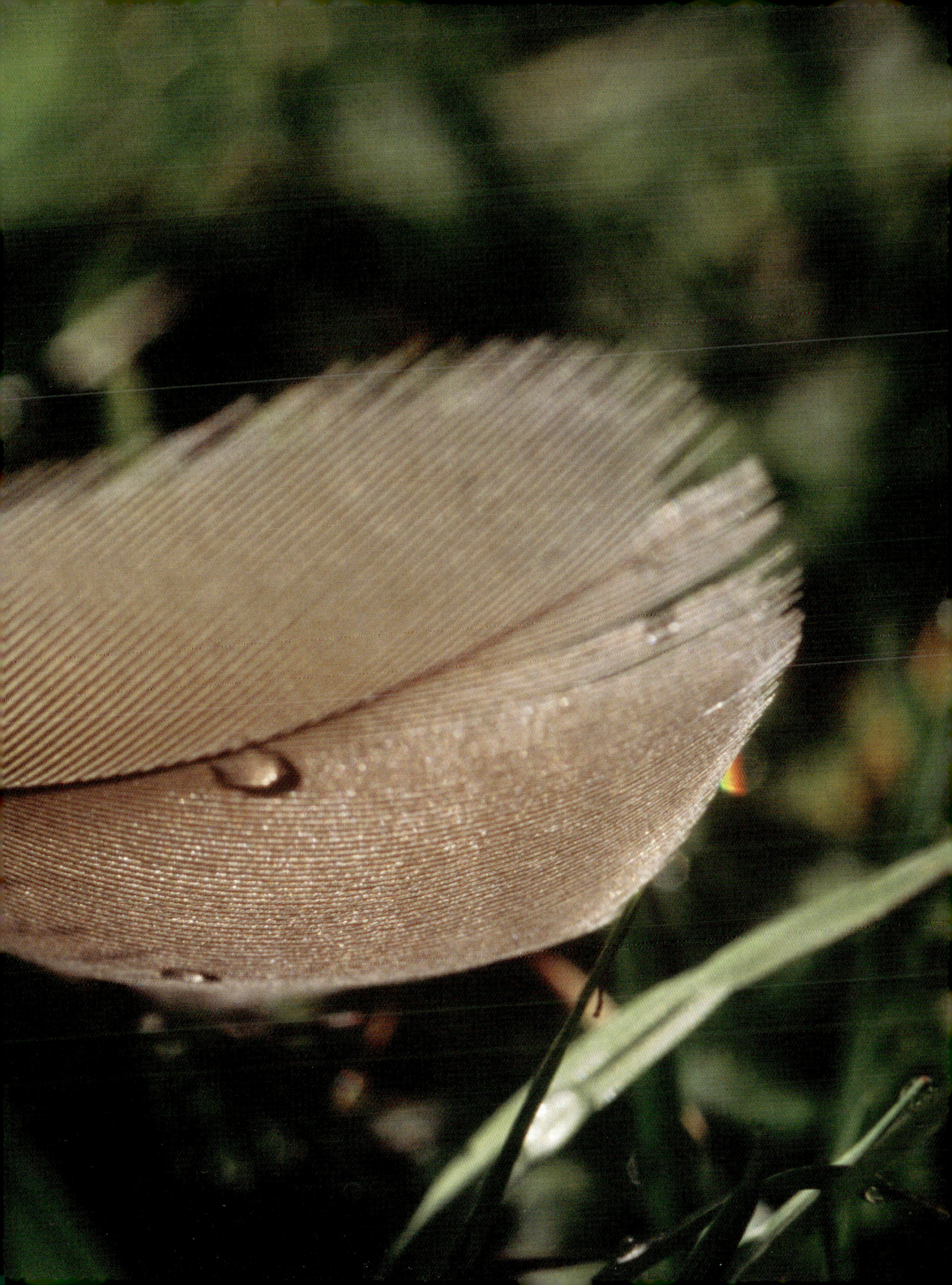

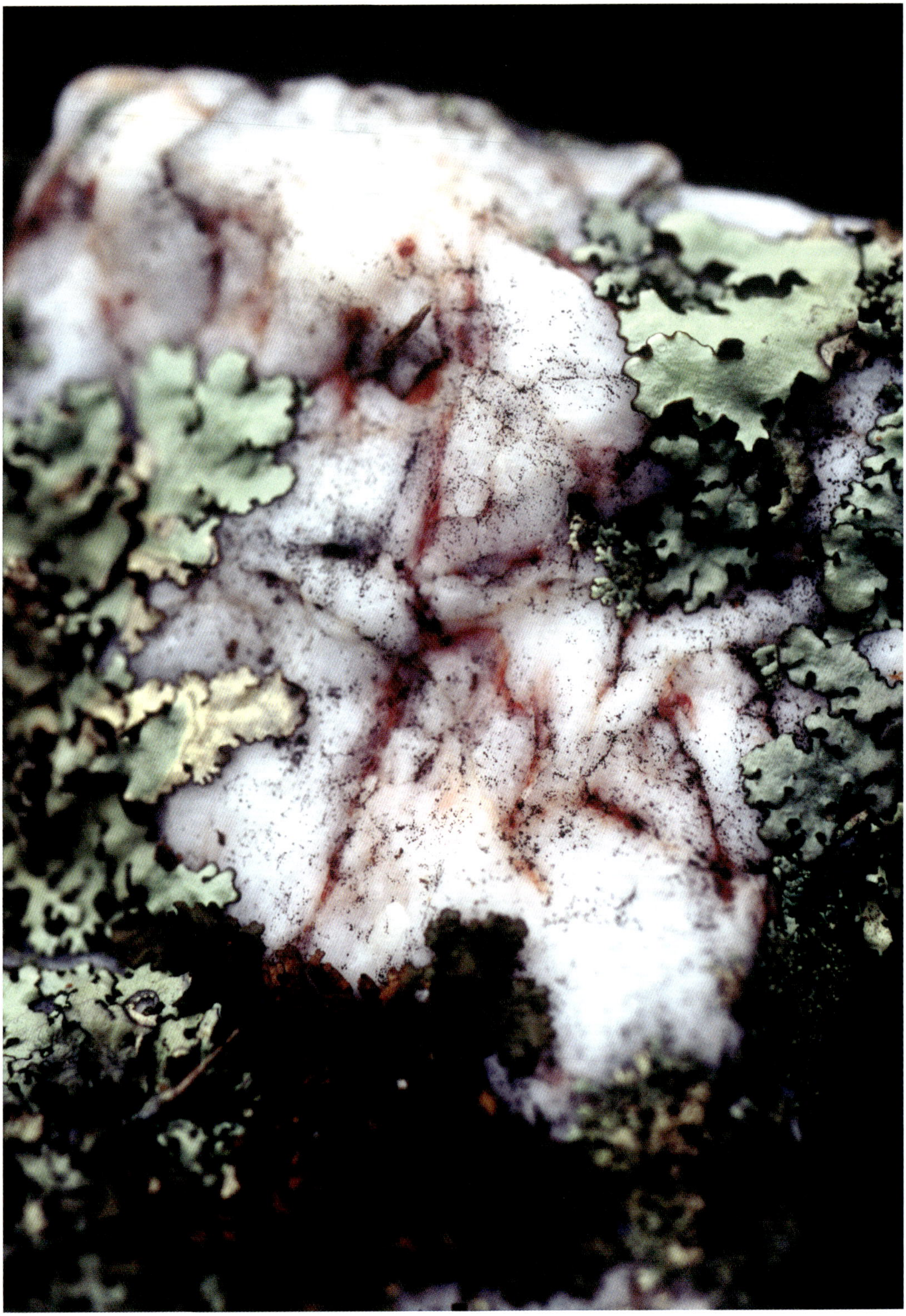

SKIN NAMES

"*Trees can be named by their healing properties, as well as their skin name. Like us, trees like to live in communities.*"

Our country extends from the highlands through the rainforest where the old grandfather and grandmother trees live. The angophoras are often called the grannies while the rough old banskias are the grandfather trees.

Genders are throughout the forests within the trees, we were taught to recognise the gender of different trees. The trees live in the family groups, and they house different birds and animals. They take them in and give them comfort; the old trees give them homes.

My mum was like this. She would give shelter to people of our mob without having met them before. Mum would see them coming and say, 'What's your gnulli?' Gnulli means 'meat' which means your skin or skin name . The answer would come back, 'My skin name is...' whichever it was. Then from that she would say 'Ah, your grandfather is...' and they would say 'Yes. That's him.'

'Ah, I know where you're from,' she would say and then feed them and give them shelter.

Mum would always say to me, 'You got to check their skin.' Skin name is a way of showing bloodline and gives you knowledge of your family tree.

Trees have skin names too, you see. Some trees have got names based on their healing abilities. The name could be based on their bark, so you might only relate the bark to the healing property it holds. Even though the tree can have another name, you might refer only to its healing properties. That healing name becomes the skin name of that fella.

Previous page: Patterns in nature – moss and quartz. Have a look at the red lines in the quartz. These represent bloodlines, which tell us our skin names.
Right: These are spotted gums. You will find bloodwoods and ironbarks with spotted gums – all quite happy to live together in a community. Working with ironbark teaches you patience as it takes so long to do anything with it.

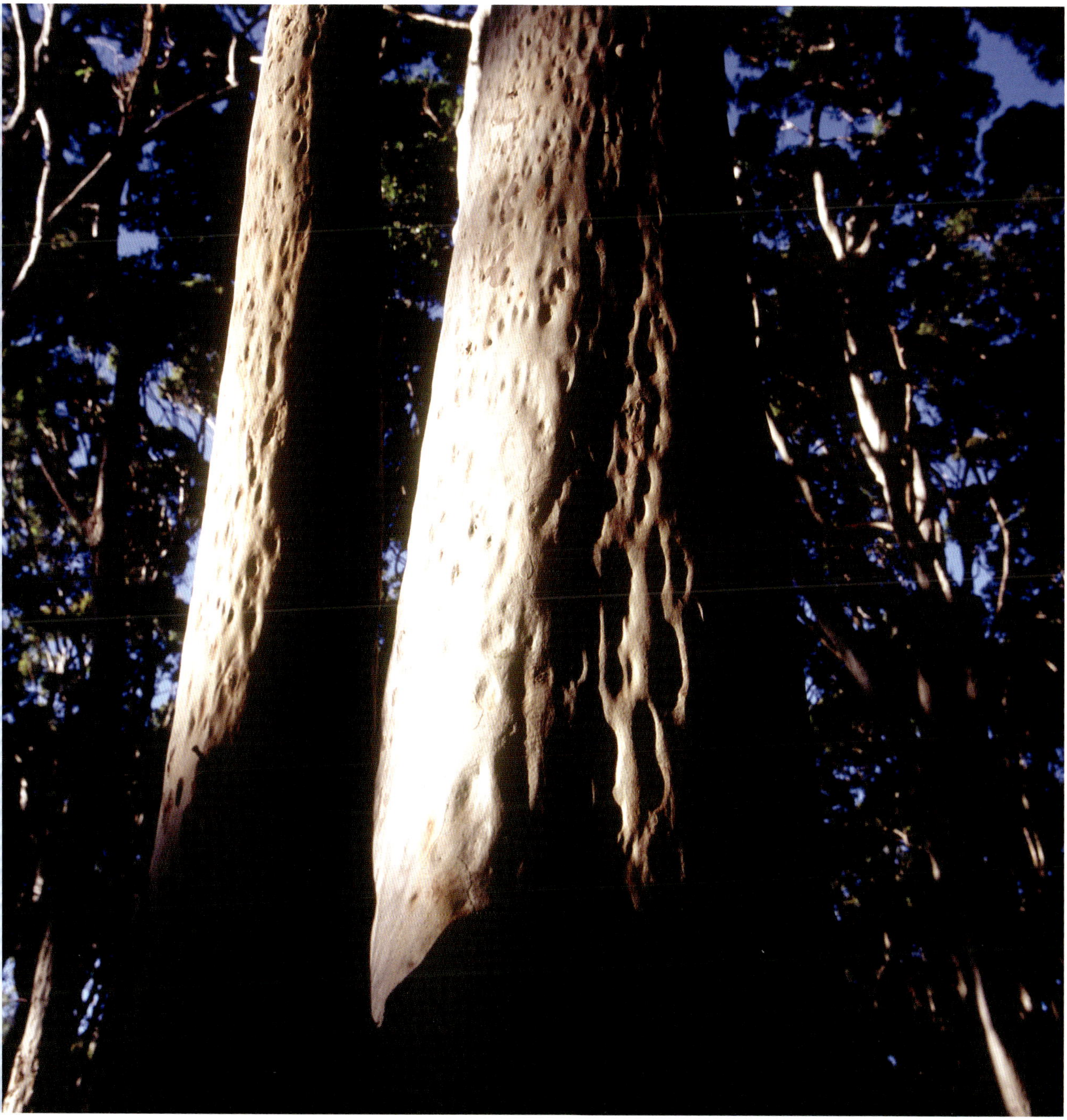

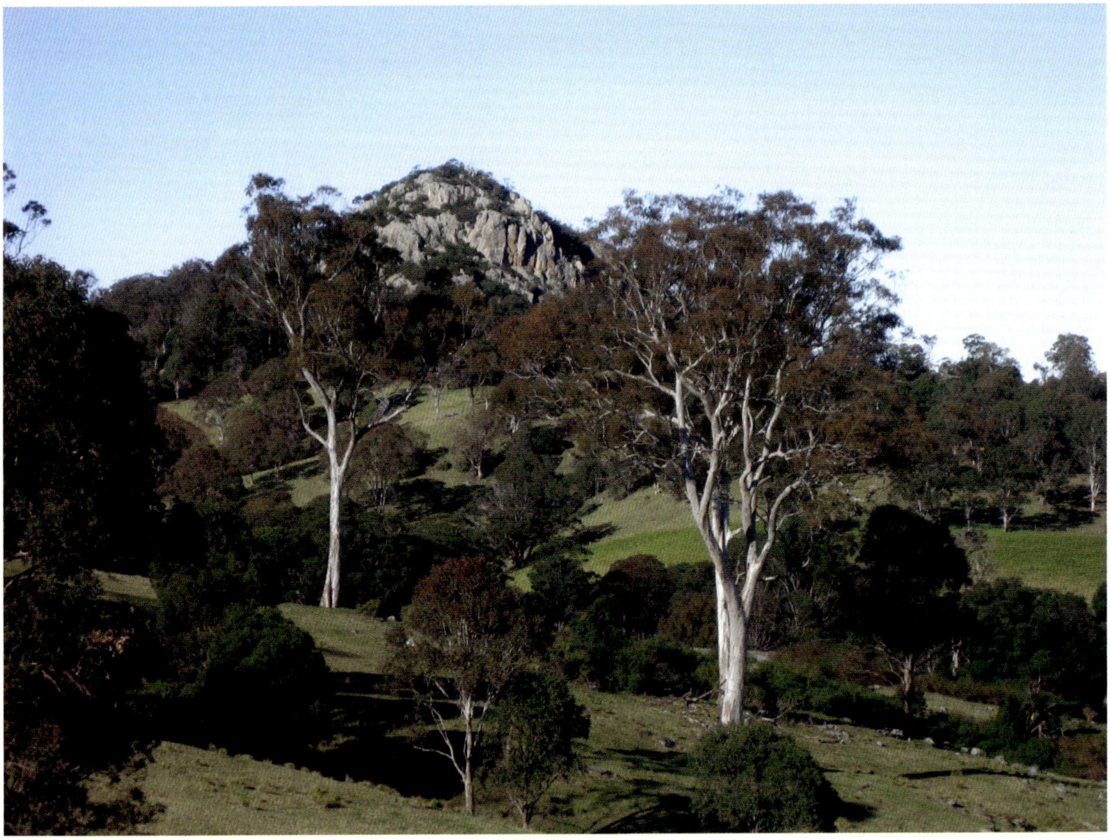

SACRED PLACES

"You often hear an old blackfella trying to say, 'That's a sacred tree' or 'That's a sacred rock,' and people telling him, 'Garbage!' People just don't understand our spiritual connectedness to the spirit of that tree, or the spirit of that water or that rock. It is so hard to explain and get people to understand our traditional practices of spirituality, our traditional practices of being in touch with our spiritual ancestors."

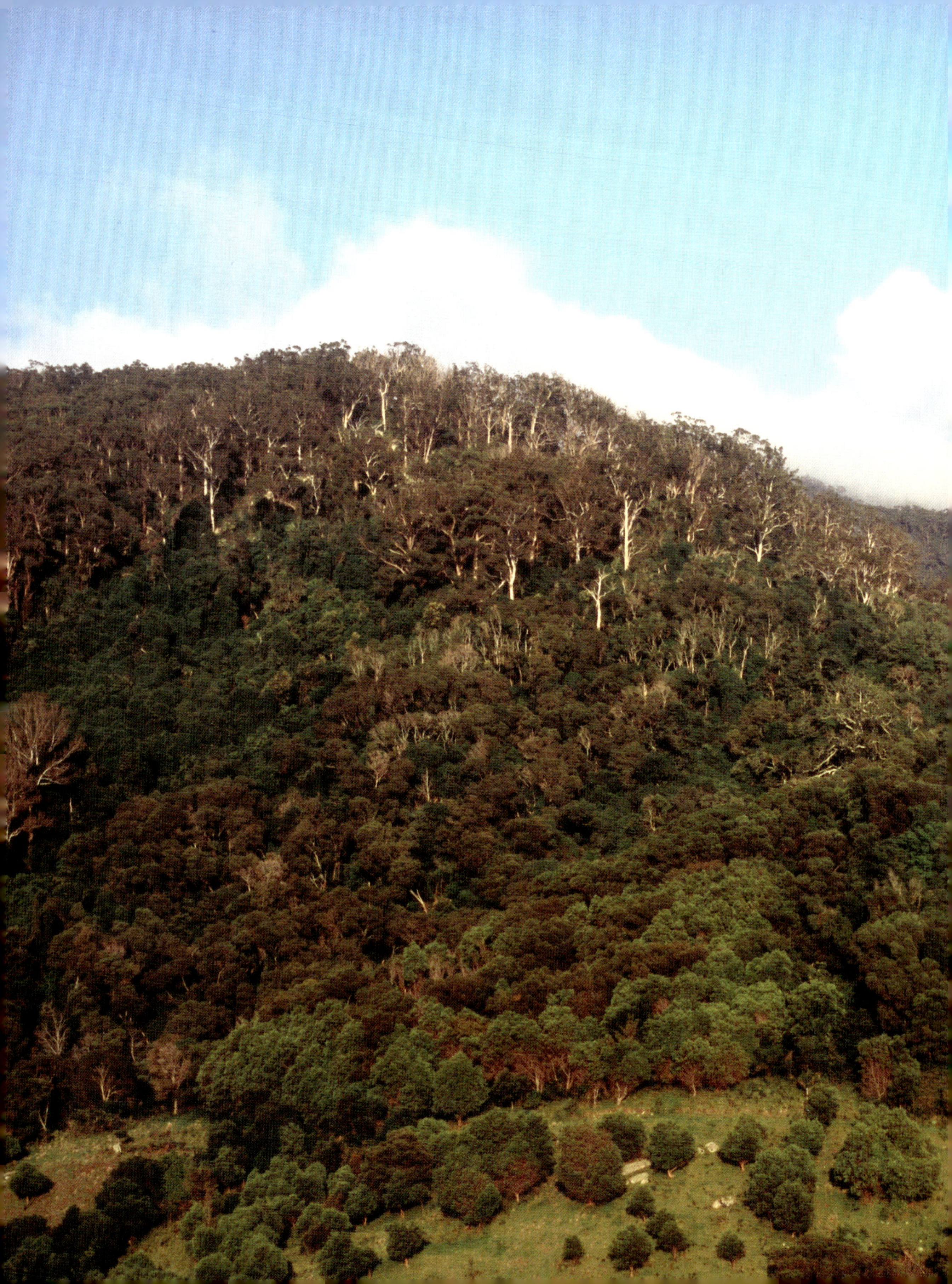

We belong to the land because Mother Earth feeds us and births everything. Non-indigenous people think they own the land, and they look on it as wealth. They start to rape that land and therefore uplift their own spirits, but the old Koori, he sings the land down and tries to hold the sacredness in the land.

Sometimes we say, 'That's a sacred place there' but because there is no evidence that it's sacred you may ask, 'How could it be sacred?' But that land has been sung: it holds the indentation, the singing, the stomping of the feet, the rhythm of the clapsticks. Down here in Yuin country there are many places where the indentation of the singing and dancing that went on over thousands of years is still evident today. Hundreds and thousands of years of stamping those old black feet as the women and the men would be passing through from circle to circle have left their mark. These circles are called Bora Rings. Some circles are 40 to 50 feet in diameter. They're huge. Then there's the little one where the children would imitate their parents, their Elders, uncles and aunties.

We dance in circles in an anticlockwise movement. I do this within ceremony today as it takes us back to the beginning. Never lose touch of your past.

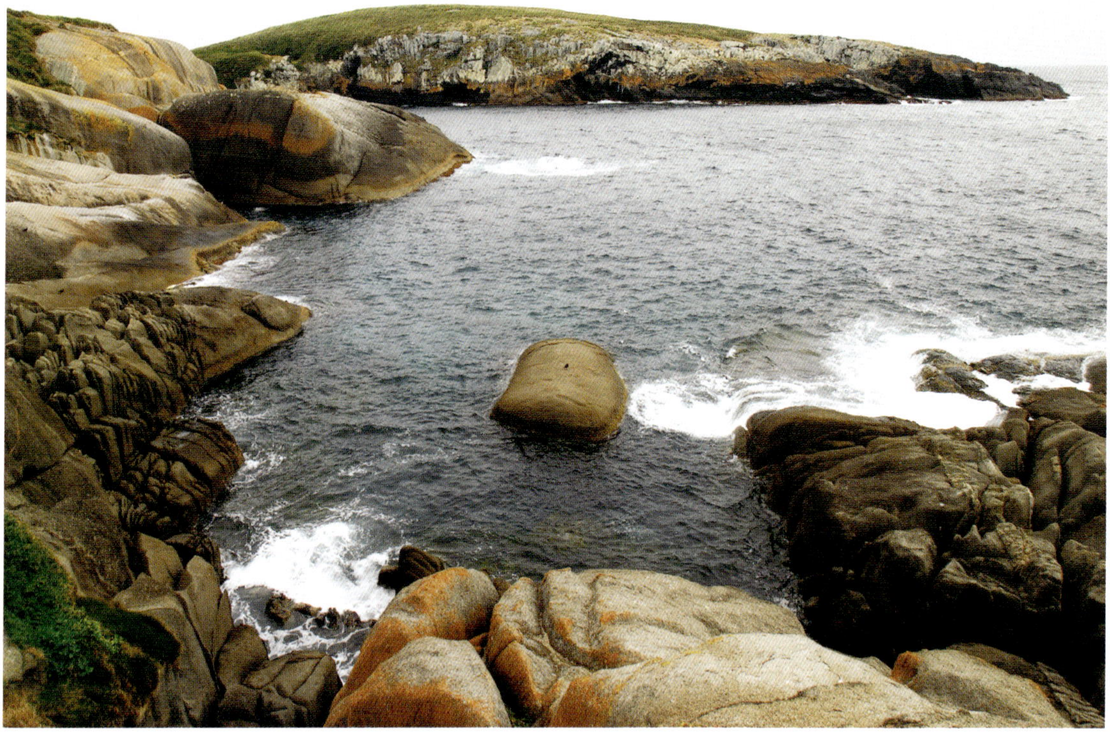

Barran-guba Island

"Barran-guba is significant to our mob because of the initiation ceremonies that were done there. There are many places of sacredness on Barran-guba where ceremonies took place."

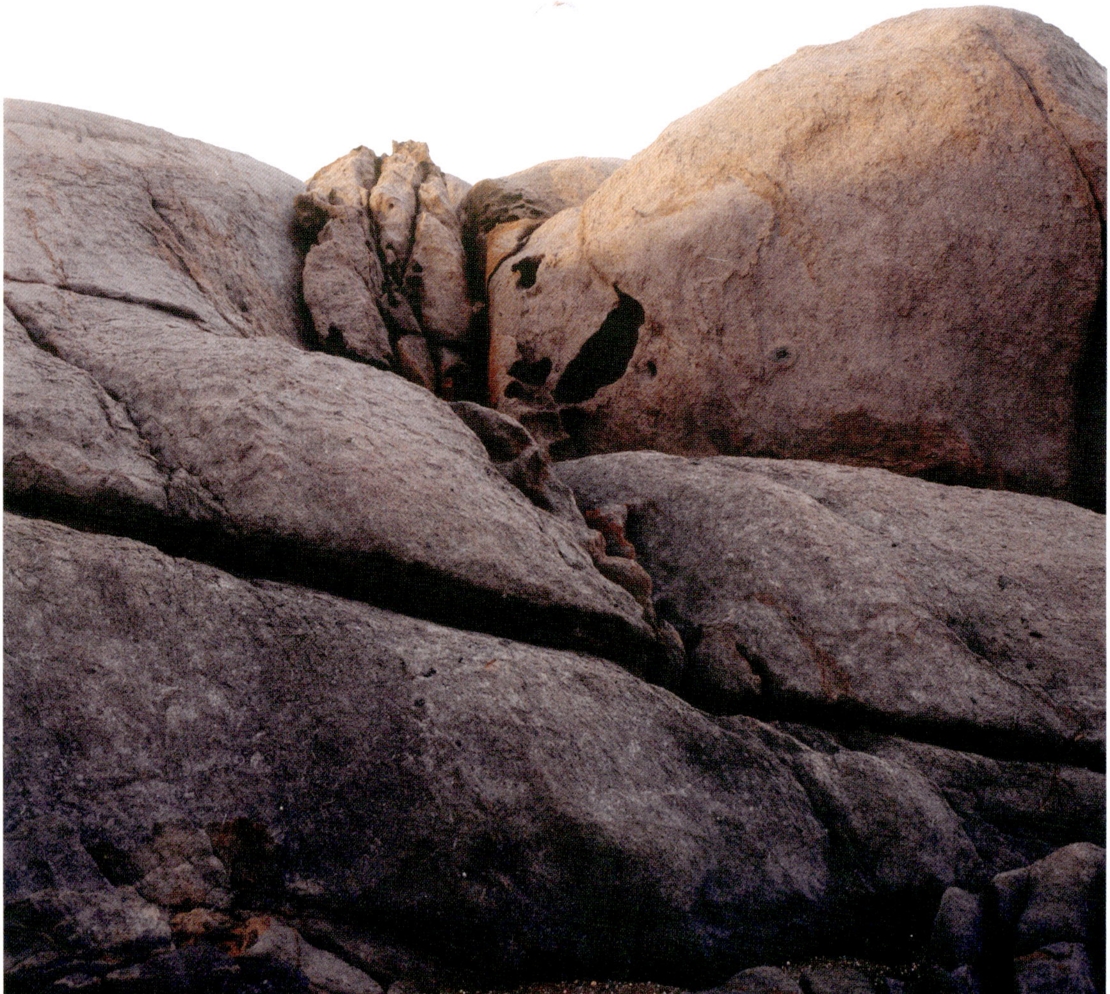

Barran-guba Island is situated about 9 kilometres off Narooma on the far south coast of New South Wales. Barran-guba is the traditional name but it is also known as Montague Island. It is the son of Gulaga Mountain. From Barran-guba Island you can also see Barran-guba's little brother, Nudganuga.

In the beginning, during the Dreamtime, someone had to come out of Gadu (ocean) to look after the food and medicines that were all up and down the coast of the Yuin Nation. A lot of the whales and dolphins were Elders too, and they were also looking for someone to be the keeper of Gadu and Barran-guba.

Barran-guba wanted to go out into Gadu and hold the Law of the sea and look after all the food and medicines. So the Koorah Koo-rie wind spirit blew and pushed Barran-guba out to sea. Barran-guba then settled at sea and began to look after the fish and medicines that were all around it. Gadu gives everything we need to take from it.

Initiation on Barran-guba usually took ten days; one day for thinking and reflecting and nine days to represent the birthing cycle, the birth of the new moon.

Previous page: The coastline of Barran-guba Island, also known as Montague Island, near Narooma, on the south coast of New South Wales. Initiation ceremonies here involved bloodletting and learning how to work with Koorah Koo-rie wind spirit.

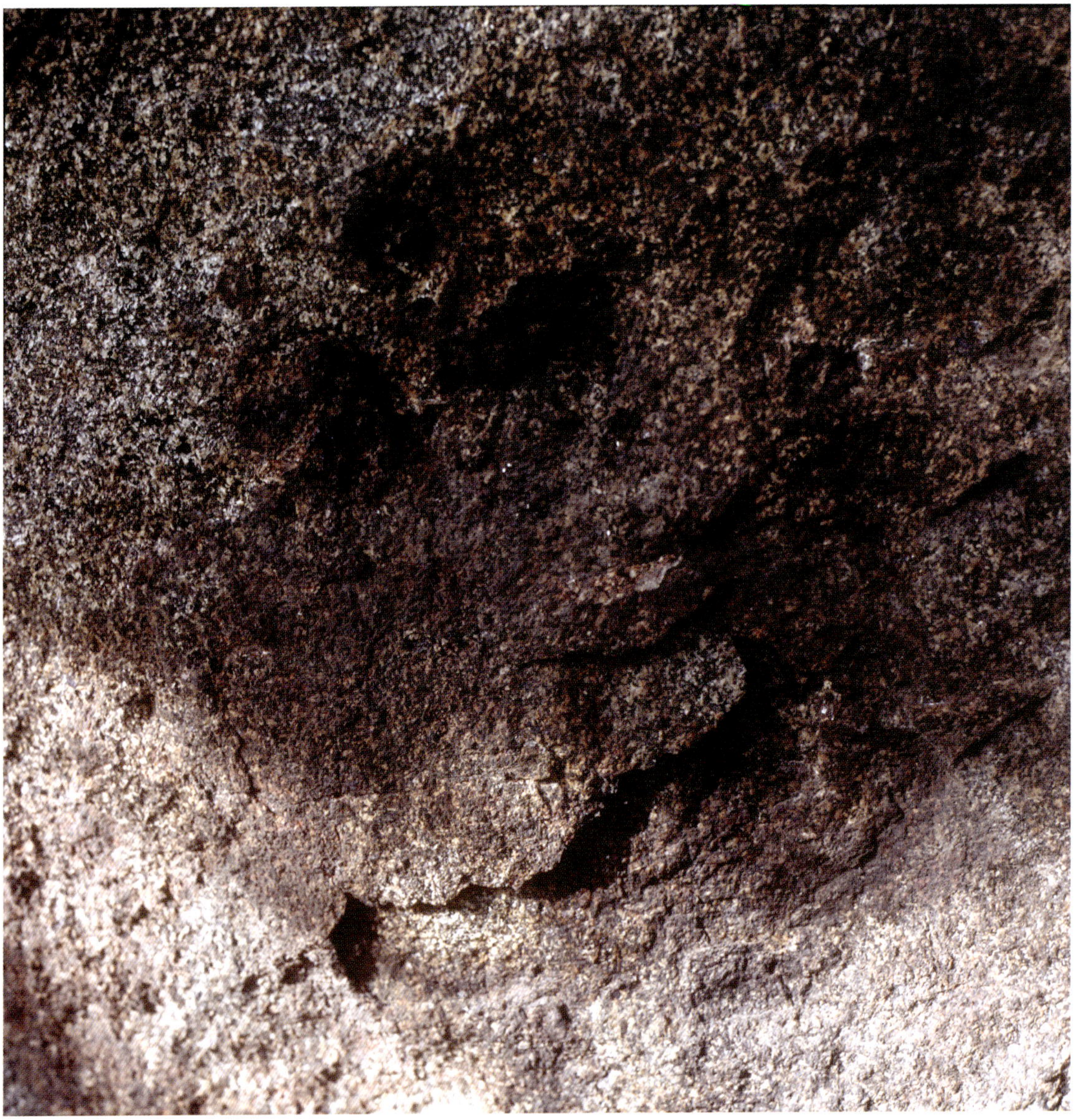

The spirits are still on Barran-guba. We are glad they are still here, they're still the guides, they are still the keepers of this place. We flesh people can come and go from here, but the spirits are here all the time, they are the true guardians of places such as Barran-guba Island.

When you are on the island you must keep your distance from the sacred places, the rocks and other pieces that have settled here, you know. You must practise your respect Laws, keep your distance and wait for the right and respectable time to travel through an area.

It's important not to be too loud and stir up the ancients [*spirits*] they will soon let you know! Or the ancients will pay you a visit, because they're here at peace and they will show up. Feel the movement and the closeness of the spirits here. The only thing to pay is respect; it's a free gift. I could never ask for a better gift than the presence of an Elder that has crossed over thousands of years ago. It's such a wonderful thing to have.

A spirit face on Barran-guba Island.

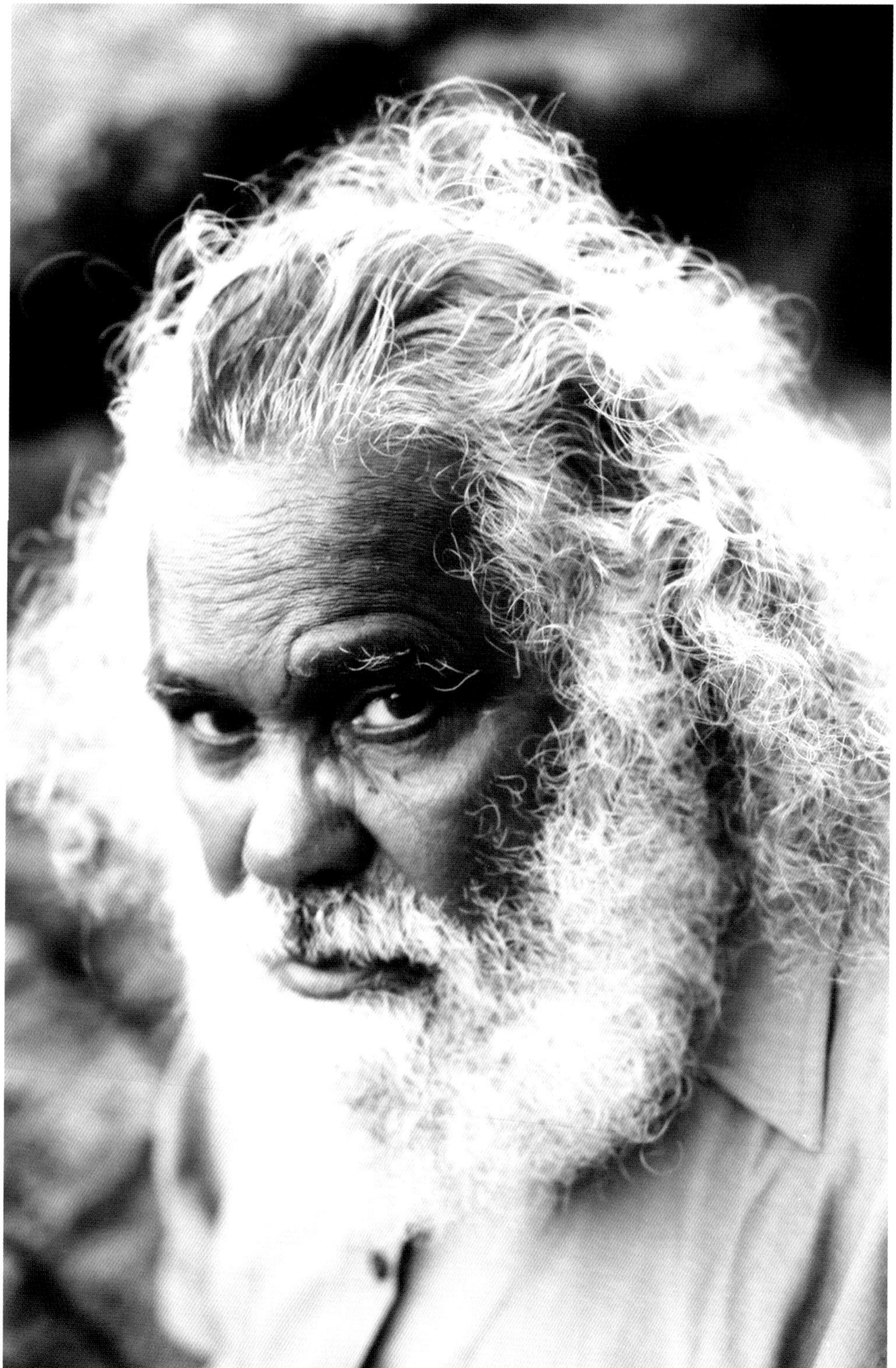

INITIATION

"*Initiation is when a boy becomes a man. You become aware of the messages the land is sending you and you feel a responsibility towards the land. You feel significantly different once you are initiated.*"

Initiation usually lasts about ten days. It can be done on Barran-guba or on the land. Initiation is about showing young boys how to be men, instilling in them how important it is to be connected to the land and to nature, to their heritage and culture.

When we do initiation on Barran-guba, the day that we arrive is familiarisation with the island, understanding where to go and where not to. There are never any questions asked, because the boys know they have to hold the Law of respect.

If someone wants to go fishing they go in threes or fours to support each other, watch over one another. The old spirits are still on this island. They're here, because they have been sung into this land, they have been sung into these rocks, the chanting that went on here, the singing, has indented their sound into the land.

People look at me when I say this; that the spirits are in the land, in the rocks and the trees and in the waters. People ask, 'But how?'. I find that a bit hard to believe. Tell me this, how could you pick up a telephone, a landline phone or a mobile phone, and talk to someone across the world or thousands of kilometres away from here? How can you record and play music? It is only technology that gives you that ability. Our people use this ability spiritually.

How can you sit down in front of a square thing with a bit of glass in front of it, such as a computer, and get images and sound out of that? Why don't you find that hard to believe? And yet when I talk about singing the land and putting voice into rocks I get queried and I think, 'Why? What's the difference between this technology and the ancient ways of communication?'

Right: Putting the red headband on to show respect for the land and the spirits.
Following page: Teaching my grandsons on Barran-guba.

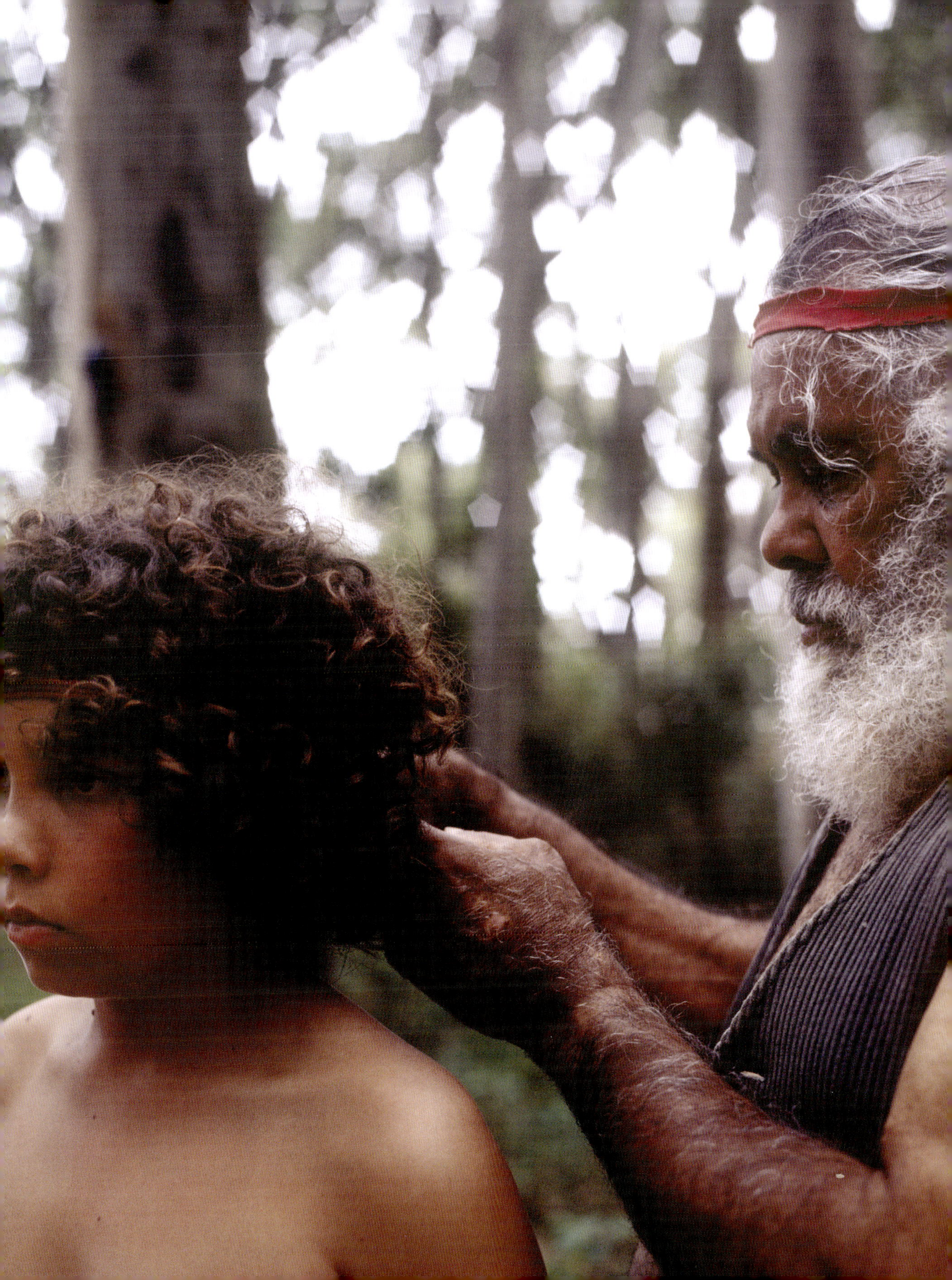

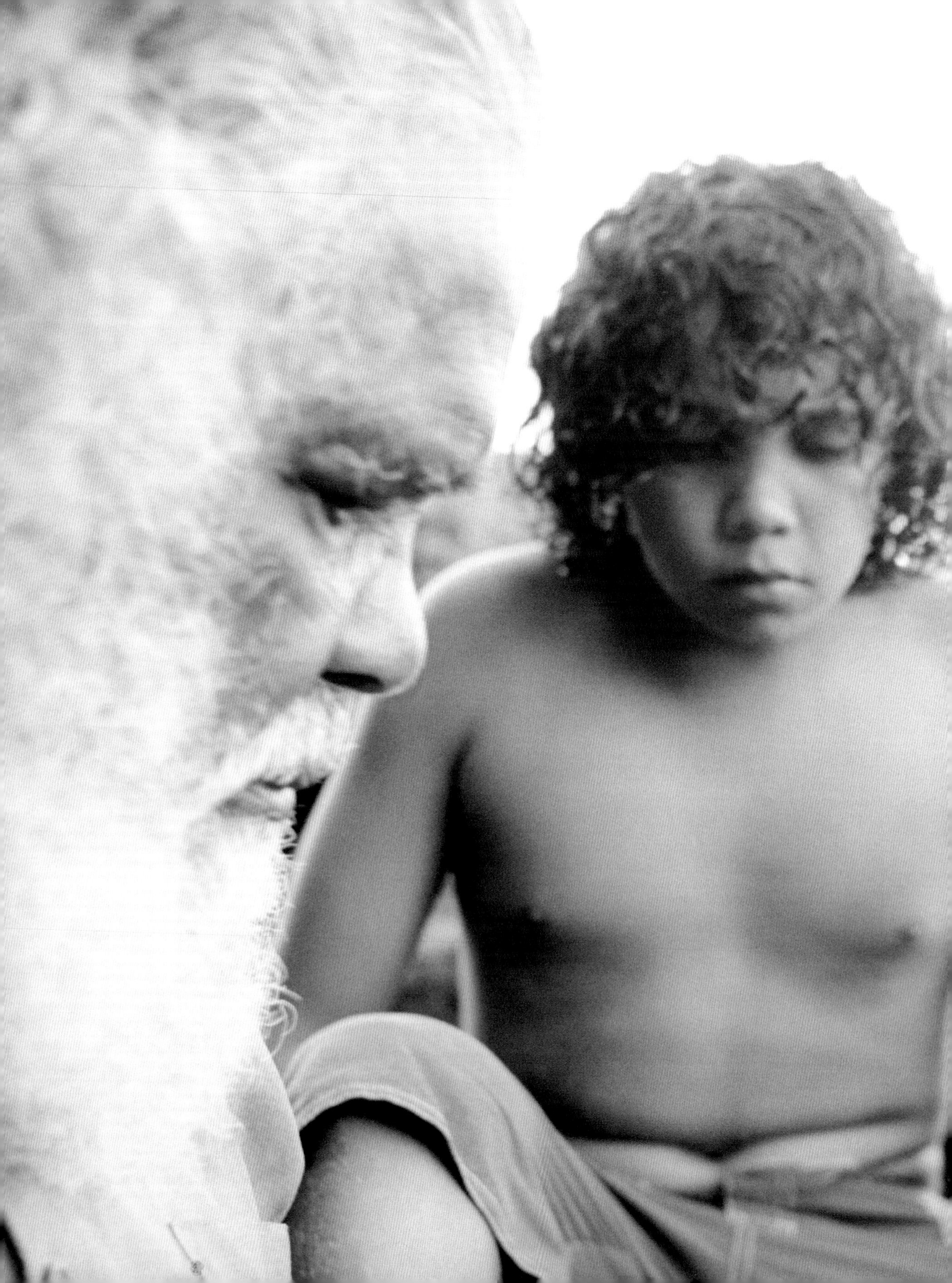

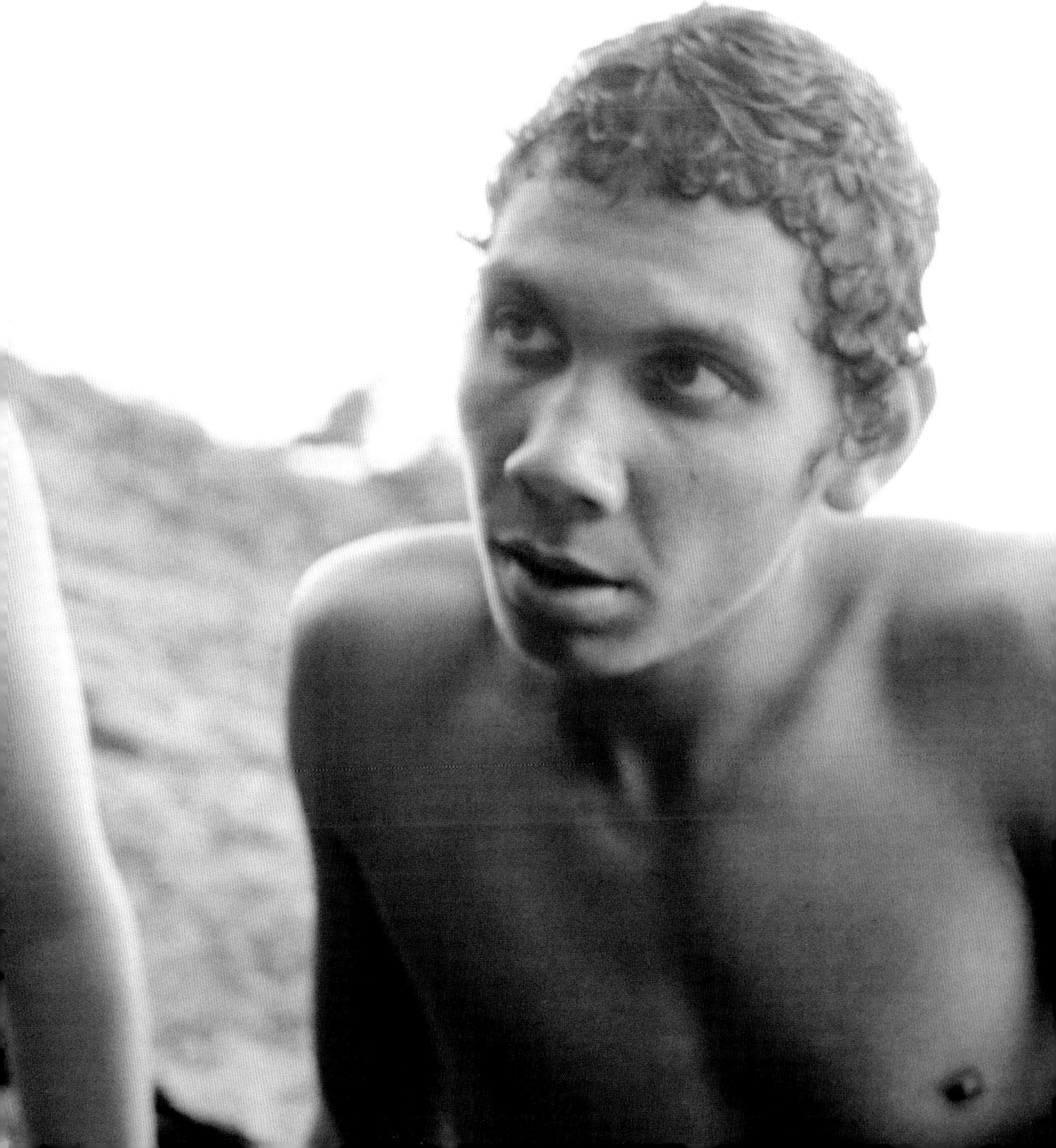

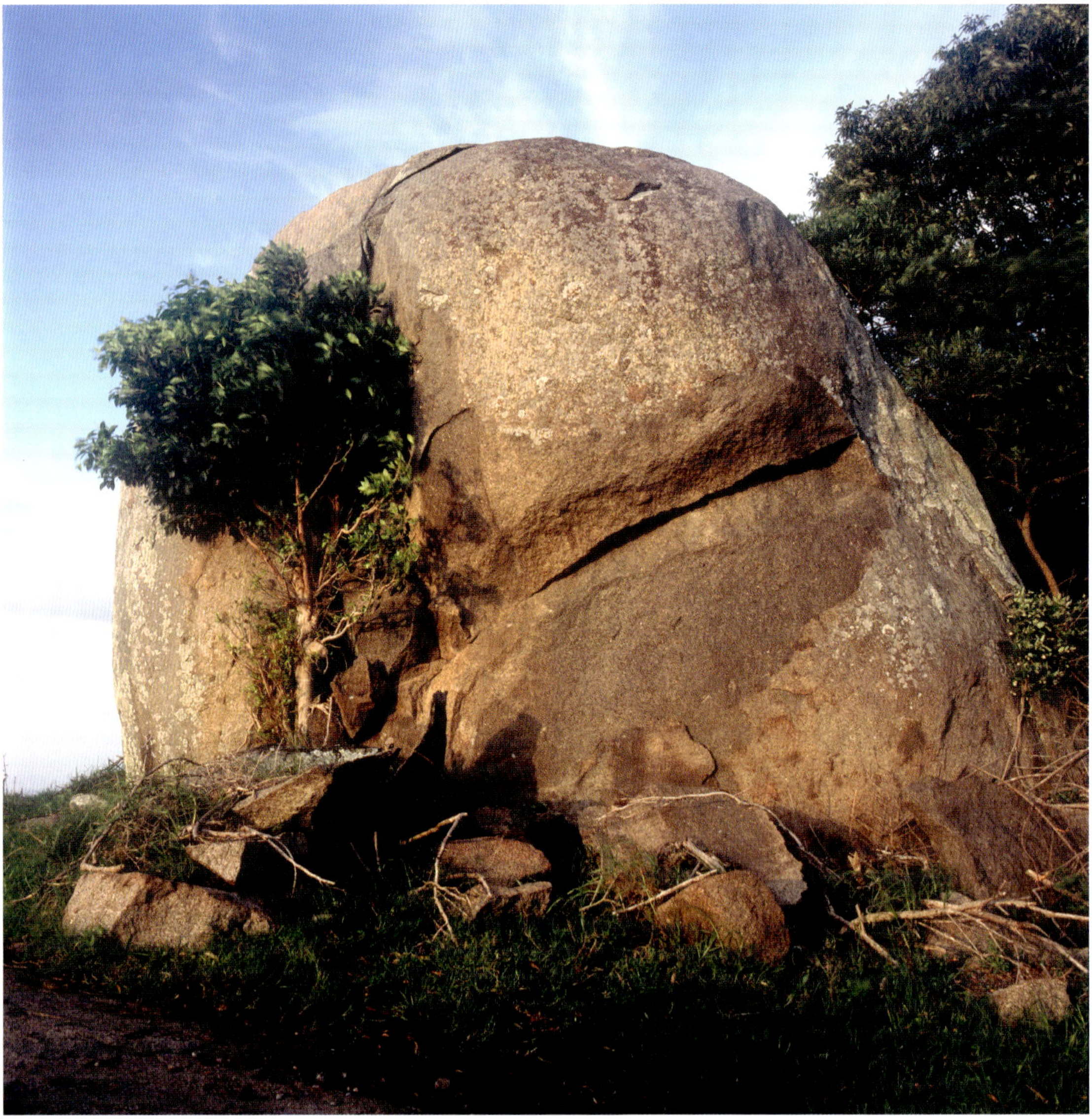

The location in initiation is so important. The calling of the ceremony is so important. When you're called into a ceremony, you go. When you get to these places of callings and look at the landscape and see the rocks and the trees, the wonderful thing you see is the land talking to you – and the shapes are giving you identification of your particular ceremony that you are going through.

Initiations belong to all ages of the male, not just from the boy to the man. The young ones are striving for their cultural and spiritual beings, their genealogy that is awakening can be frightening until they sit with the Elders and they set them straight.

I feel sad that there is no initiation with non-indigenous people. Spiritual connectedness is so important with a tree or water or a bay near the ocean. If you connect with them, they become significant to you. Don't look at the (money) value of the land, look at the spiritual aspect of the land – and by doing so look at what the land can give you. When it's about money, it's got to be ripped from the ground. If you look at wealth differently you will understand Mother Earth is such an important thing.

This connectedness to the land, this ritual of initiating young boys to men, is something that white people also can feel and understand, if they see and feel that everything is connected. Everyone gets everything from Mother Earth, no matter what. It's born from her, and if you understand that you can have a sacred knowledge, not a secret knowledge, but a sacred knowledge of the land. Once you start connecting with the Mother, it gives you a feeling of 'Whoa, I can now see the importance of Aboriginal survival of 80,000 years' heritage.' They can also see how it's been wiped away by modern stuff like bulldozers and ploughs and infrastructure. Making our backyards look beautiful, beautifying them with all the stones and the sticks and the pebbles.

No Aboriginal woman is allowed on Barran-guba Island. It is forbidden. We came to the island through the magnificent craftsmanship of the canoe makers. These canoes would hold up to between 11 and 17 men; they were huge. Out on Barran-guba you have got seafood and nothing else. It is very different to initiation done on the land. If you have got first-timers you are always best to have a lot of Elders there with you, senior sort of guys, but the boys' initiation is not so intense as on the land.

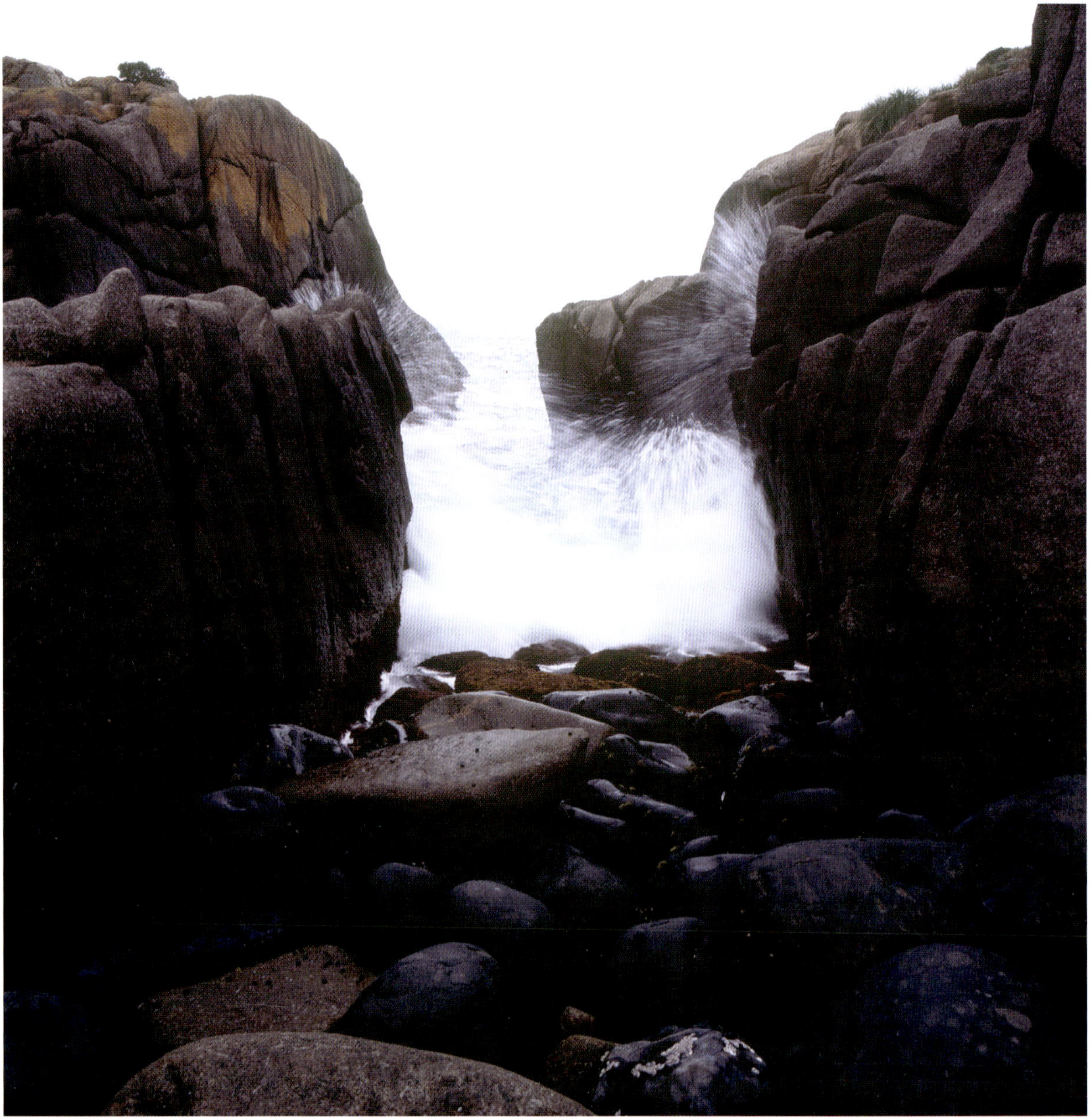

What people don't understand is that when some of these landscape artists gather all these things, they are not only gathering stones, they are gathering bones. So they have got stones and bones that have been dumped into their backyards, to beautify the area.

What they also don't understand is that that land where the bones have been put had been sung with ceremony. There were bodies being put into those places, and sung into the land so that they could rest. It is the same today if you walk into any church where a body is about to be buried, you will hear a hymn being sung. People are still doing that kind of performance. Yet when we say, 'Don't tear up that creek, don't tear up that part of the river, that is sacred, ceremony was done there,' people don't hear. If we can get people to understand that and let them connect spiritually to the land, then they will start to understand.

The initiations on Barran-guba were all bloodletting and disciplinary, and the perfection of how these ceremonies were conducted with the initiates was cleverly done. This was passed on to me, which enabled me to continue the initiation ceremony on Barran-guba and hold law, keeping our traditions alive.

Bloodletting is when each young man is cut with cutting stones from their homelands. First they are taught to shear the cutting stone to make them razor sharp. Some of these sophisticated cutting stones have come from hundreds of kilometres across the mainland, and the spirits in these stones found their way here through the young initiates. Time is given, some days, for the young men to get to know their stones, to become familiar and to recognise and understand them before they stand in front of the Elders. All the young initiates' cutting stones are scattered on the ground together on the day of the beginning of the initiation. The young men then take their stones; by now they know them well. What follows after that remains sacred to the young men who have been through this law.

To this day our initiations continue, the bloodletting flows, the boy comes out and the man begins. That is so important: this is for manhood.

When we take the boys out to Barran-guba we don't allow them to go on the eastern side of the island because the rocks are so slippery and you can't get up. Then you get exhausted trying to get around to the gap or to swim back down around to the southern part of it. Besides that, there's the sharks that are just around, all waiting there with the seals and the penguins. You have got half of the island to do your gathering, and very little hunting. So the initiation is about the gathering of fish, seafood, seashells and shellfish. It's a pretty disciplined thing because the boys learn to look at the elements such as the wind, which is an important factor on the island. Most times Barran-guba is not the first initiation for the boys, unless you want to do a hard, fast one.

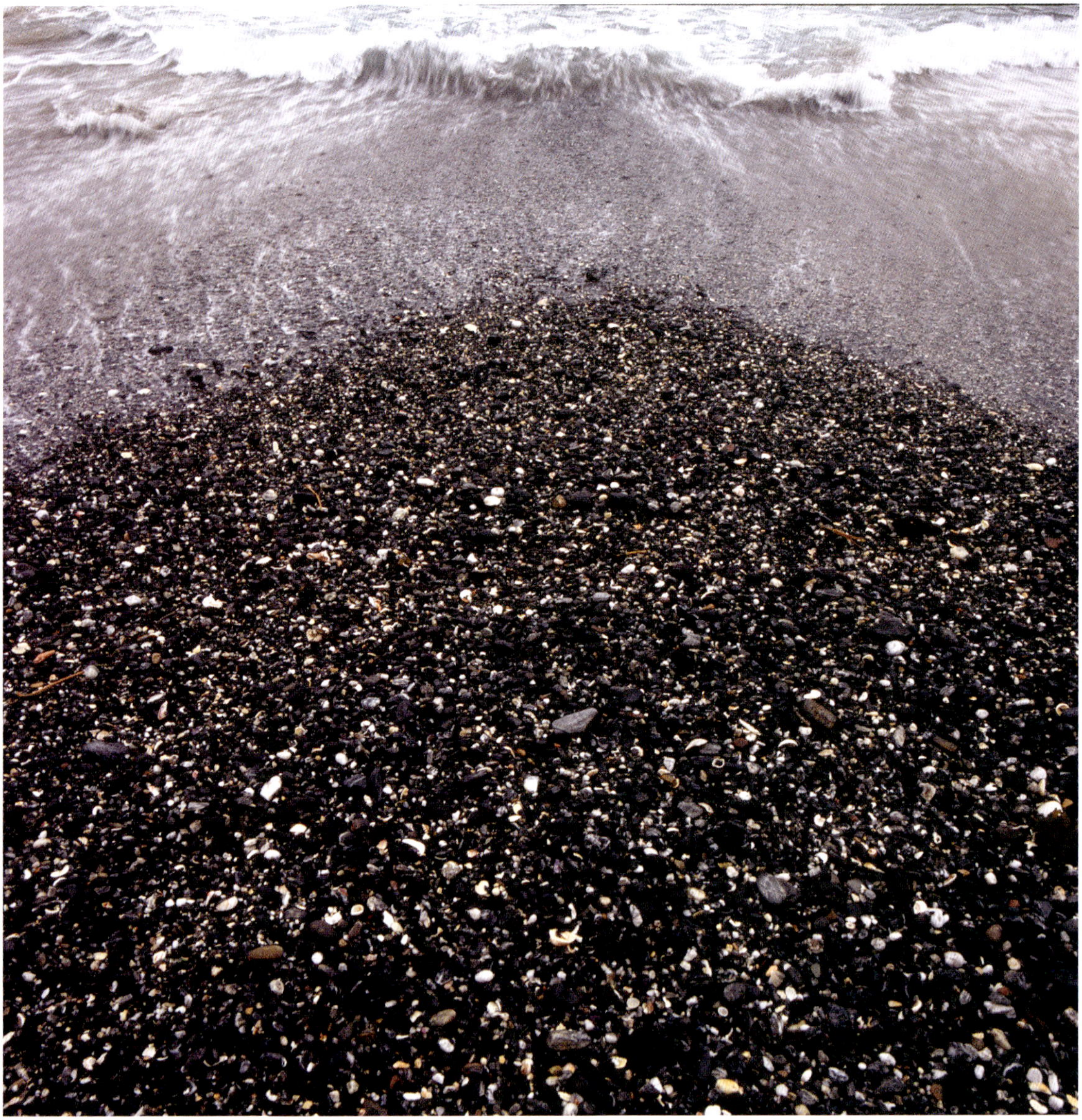

DEATH AND BURIAL

"*It's true of most funerals that when people go into a church they are singing a song. They call it hymns. The singing into the ground; singing into the rocks; singing into the water; the indentation of that spiritual stuff – those are our hymns. People can be scared of death because they think it is final, but we know it is not. People go on living after their flesh body has died. The bodies of the dead are just the suitcases for the spirit, which keeps on being with us.*"

Our people are buried according to lore, facing east, to see the first sunrise of each day. Even in death, as in life, we greet Grandfather Sun each day.

Usually, at a traditional burial, there are four sticks placed in the ground. The first is placed in the east, the second in the west, the third in the south and the fourth in the north. The grave is dug off-centre from the east and west and off-centre from the north and south. When the body is carried in, it is always brought in from the east, the place of the first sunrise, along a winding track. Smoke is lit at different points along the track. The body is placed in the grave and people follow the body along the track and gather round in a circle. As they stand there they do their ceremonial mourning, they create their rebirth. As the dead person is coming down the track another life is coming in.

When I saw my mother was sick, I panicked as I had never seen her ill before. I organised all the grandchildren and great-grandchildren together; they came from all over. It was something I thought was important because Mum was so ill. Five generations of family were there. Over 100 people came to be there with Mum. I thought it was our last feast with her. Then I noticed Mum sitting down, holding one of the babies. I walked over to her, her eyes were closed, she was just rocking and humming with that baby. I said to her, 'Who's that boori you got in your arms?' Mum's words rocked me. She said, 'Oh, I don't know but it's me.' What she was saying was that she would live on as long as her descendents kept breeding.

Previous page: A beach on the south coast of New South Wales which is sacred to the Yuin people. The thousands of highly polished rocks represent the souls of the departed.

Right: At a traditional burial, there are four sticks placed in the ground. The first is placed in the east, the second in the west, the third in the south and the fourth in the north. The grave is dug off-centre from the east and west and off-centre from the north and south. When the body is carried in, it is always brought in from the east, place of the first sunrise, along a winding track.

N

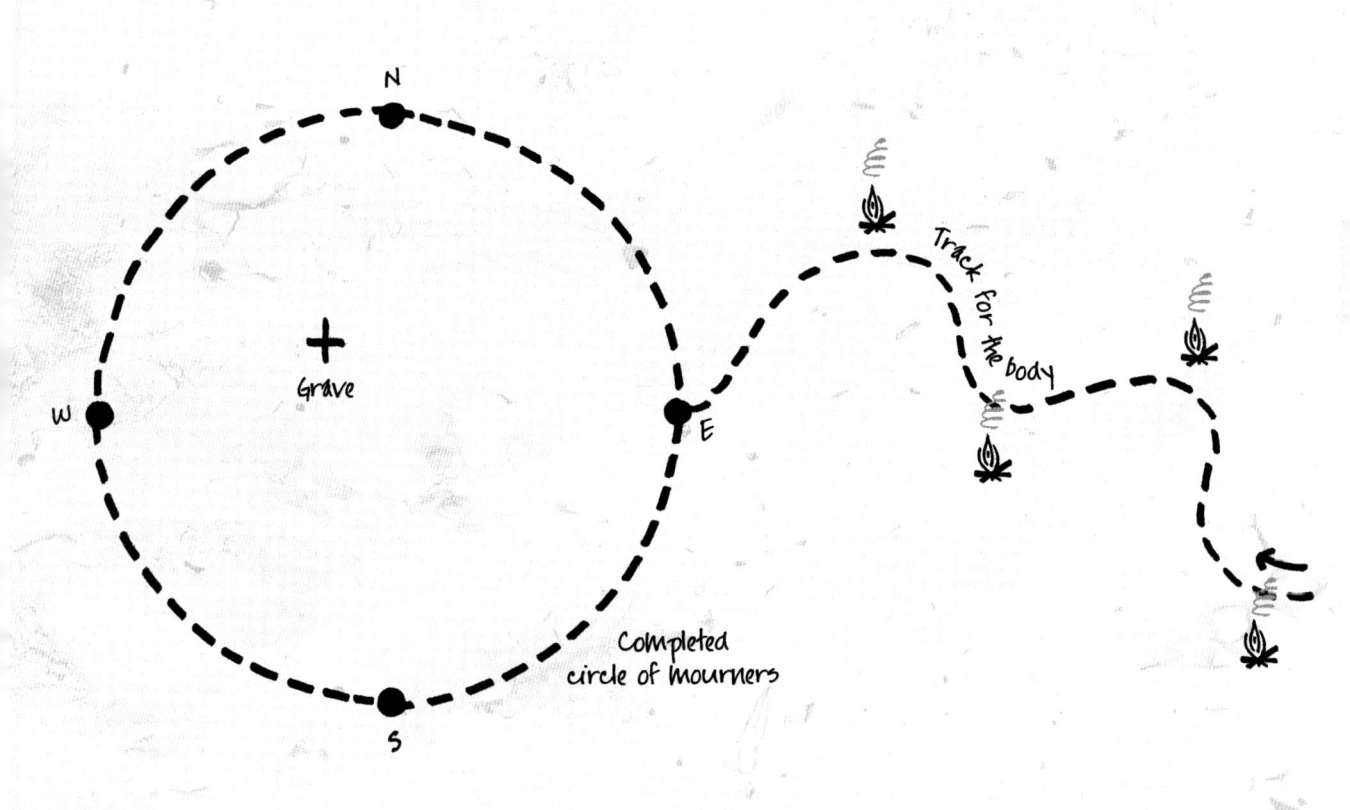

W

Grave

E

S

Completed circle of mourners

Track for the body

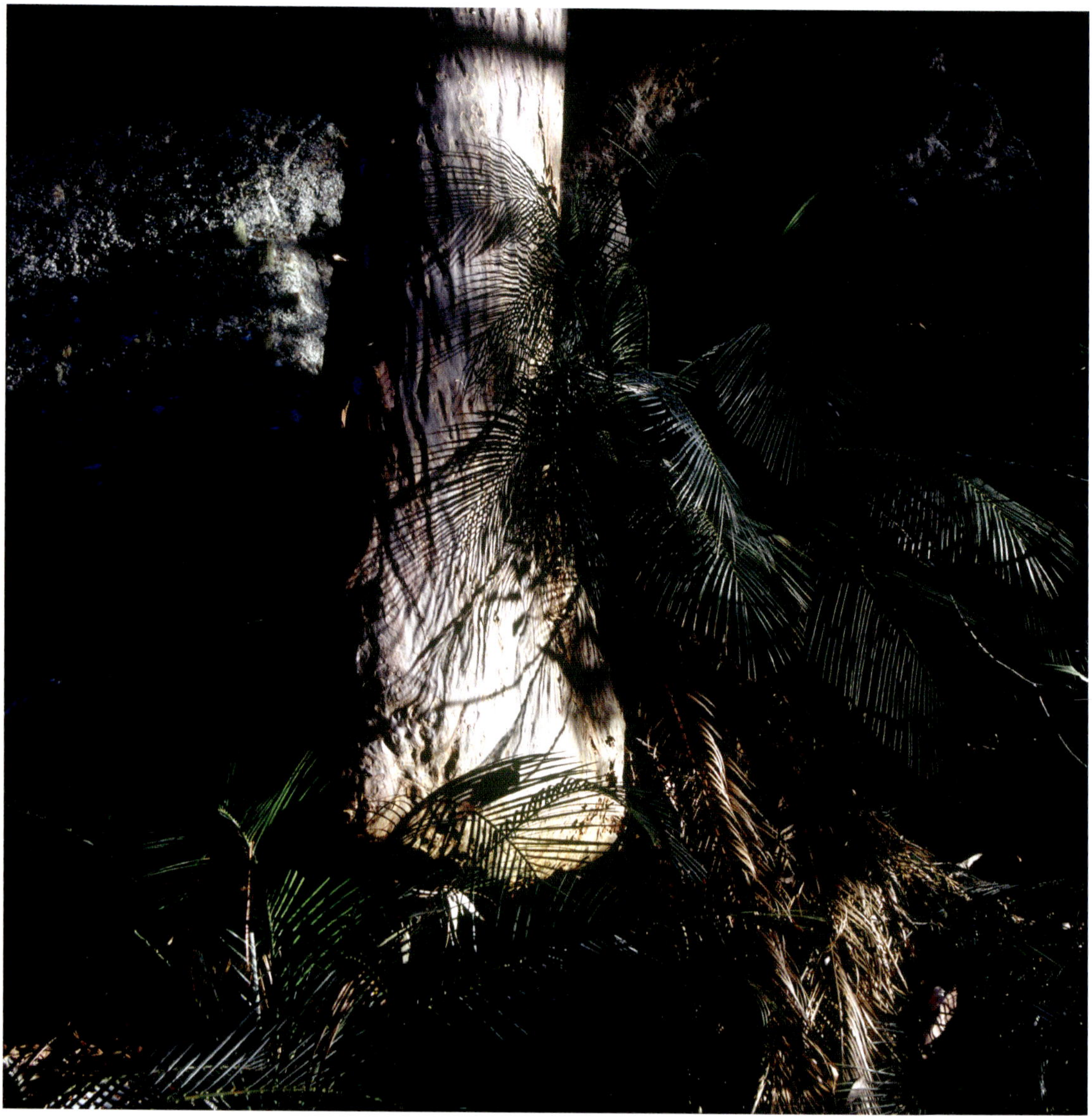

COMMUNICATING WITH THE DEAD

"Communication with the dead is the most wonderful thing. I keep understanding and I keep learning all the time. I get the knowledge and the wisdom from the spiritual Elders who just keep clipping me under the ear, you know, putting me on the right track when it comes to my teachings."

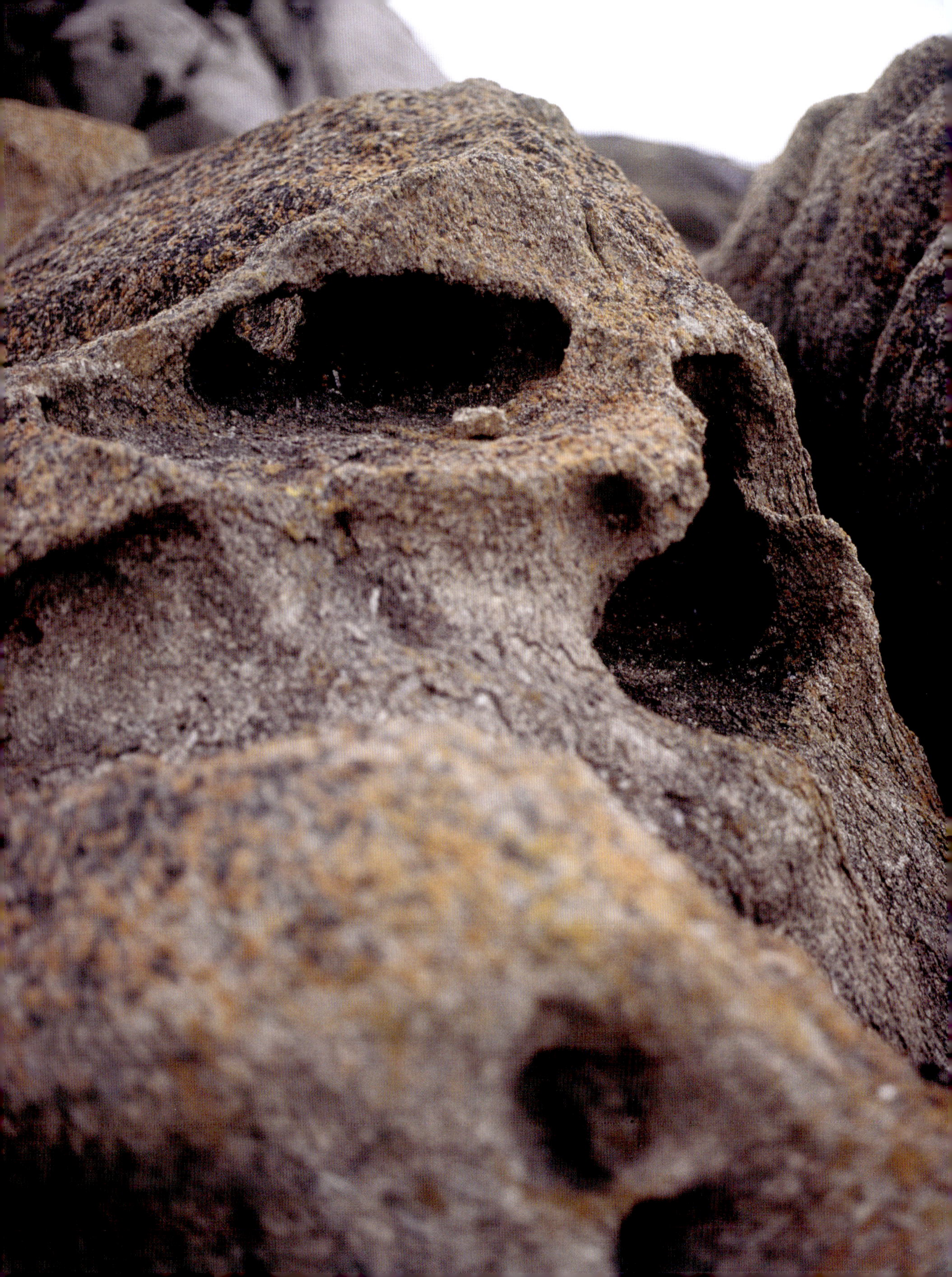

My mother lived to the age of 99, when she finally passed over, and my grandfather was 104. I still communicate with them. I enjoy communicating with the so-called dead, with those that have gone by, sitting down talking. There's lots of ways to communicate through the spiritual connectedness of the spirit that passed over.

Communicating with the dead takes fear away of this unknown. When I was a young man travelling around the country, the only safe place for me to sleep was in or around a cemetery. Not too many people would come into a cemetery at night because of their fear of the unknown, and they didn't know how to communicate with the spirit world. That was one of the most important things shown to me after I stopped going to Sunday School.

The Sunday School teachers would be talking about God. One day I asked one of the most boldest, silliest questions. I asked, 'Excuse me, but have you seen God?' There was a stutter and a stammer and the teachers said, 'No, we have never seen God, and don't ask such a silly question.' I felt so ridiculed by that reply. Then I asked my old aunties, 'Why is it that these Sunday School teachers haven't seen God?' And they said, 'Well, it's probably because they don't see spirits, and that's why they got angry with you.'

I replied, 'But they were telling me that they are the image of God and I can't understand why they call God him. Why is it that God has got to be him, and not her?' All these things raced through my mind.

I've seen people going to church over the years and praying to a being that they have not seen, and all the time not understanding that the Great Creator, the work of the Great Creator, is all around them.

There are people (spirits) that I have been communicating with for a long time. First of all I got a bit scared when I saw spirits, I got scared when I heard things, but then an old Uncle told me not to fear because that's what I was going to be one day.

The spirits show themselves in the rocks and trees in natural forms. These spirits came from the land the same as us. The spirit is in that rock, the spirit is in that tree, because its born from Mother Earth, there's no separation between us. I will show myself in a form you understand to tell you we are one, that there is a deeper story to know.

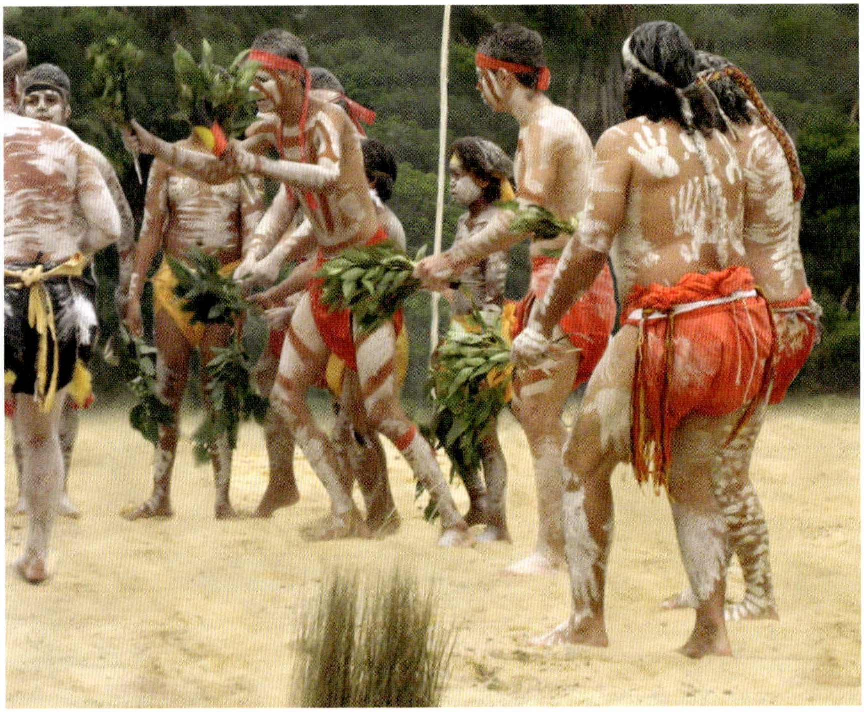

CEREMONY

"*Ceremony marks an important occasion in our life cycle.*"

When we have ceremony, the old people will go to a specific area to dance. They dance in circles, which we call Bora Rings. Bora Rings are places where you go and do performances. Some Bora Rings are ceremonial places for bloodletting and some of them for dance. Dancing is about making an indentation on the land, the sand going into the rocks, the song going into the trees, making a recording session without technology. It's spiritual connectedness to the land – to feel the earth move to your rhythm is such an important thing.

The land, the rocks, the trees, they all hold the indentation of song and movement generated from the Bora Rings. You can feel the energy move under your feet and feel it go through your body. Our people don't question this.

Modern technology comes from a flick of a switch, but our ancient culture is with the land. This new technology is where we lose touch with nature, it's disconnected from the source. We got to get back on the land, we got to walk, we got to talk, we've got to feel that sense of the natural world.

When you think you own the land it turns on you, you don't own it; it owns you. You can't take your 100 000 acres with you or put it in your pocket to re-establish itself. We think we can re-shape it, bring in rocks from somewhere else, dig up riverbeds … change nature's way to suit our ego economy.

The rocks in the distance show a place on Barran-guba where initiation ceremonies were held. The boys being initiated would form two rings or nests, with one ring made up of the boys going to be initiated and the other made up of boys who had been initiated. It is quite a walk to get to the initiation spot, lots of grass and rocky terrain to cover, although it looks quite easy here.

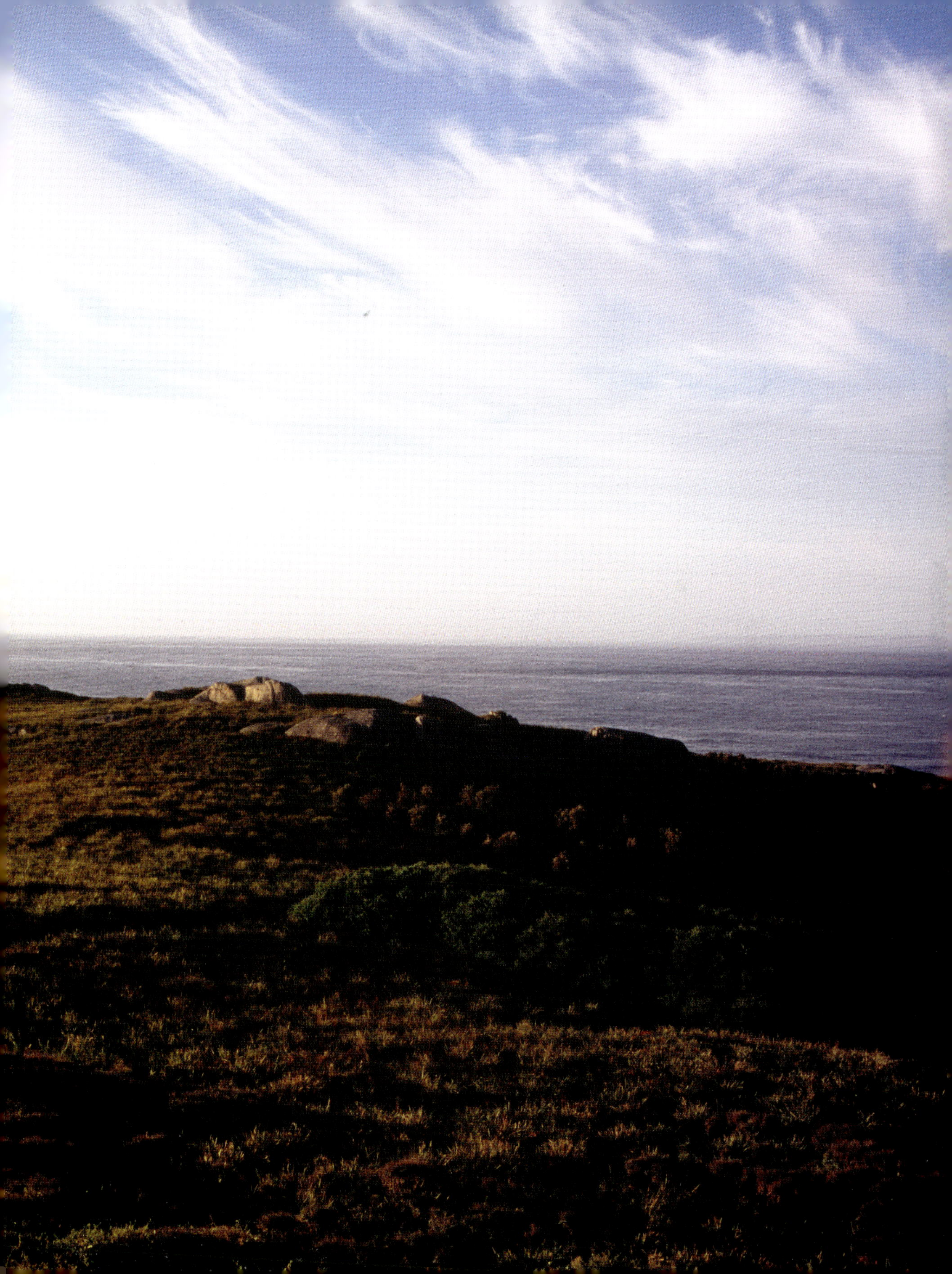

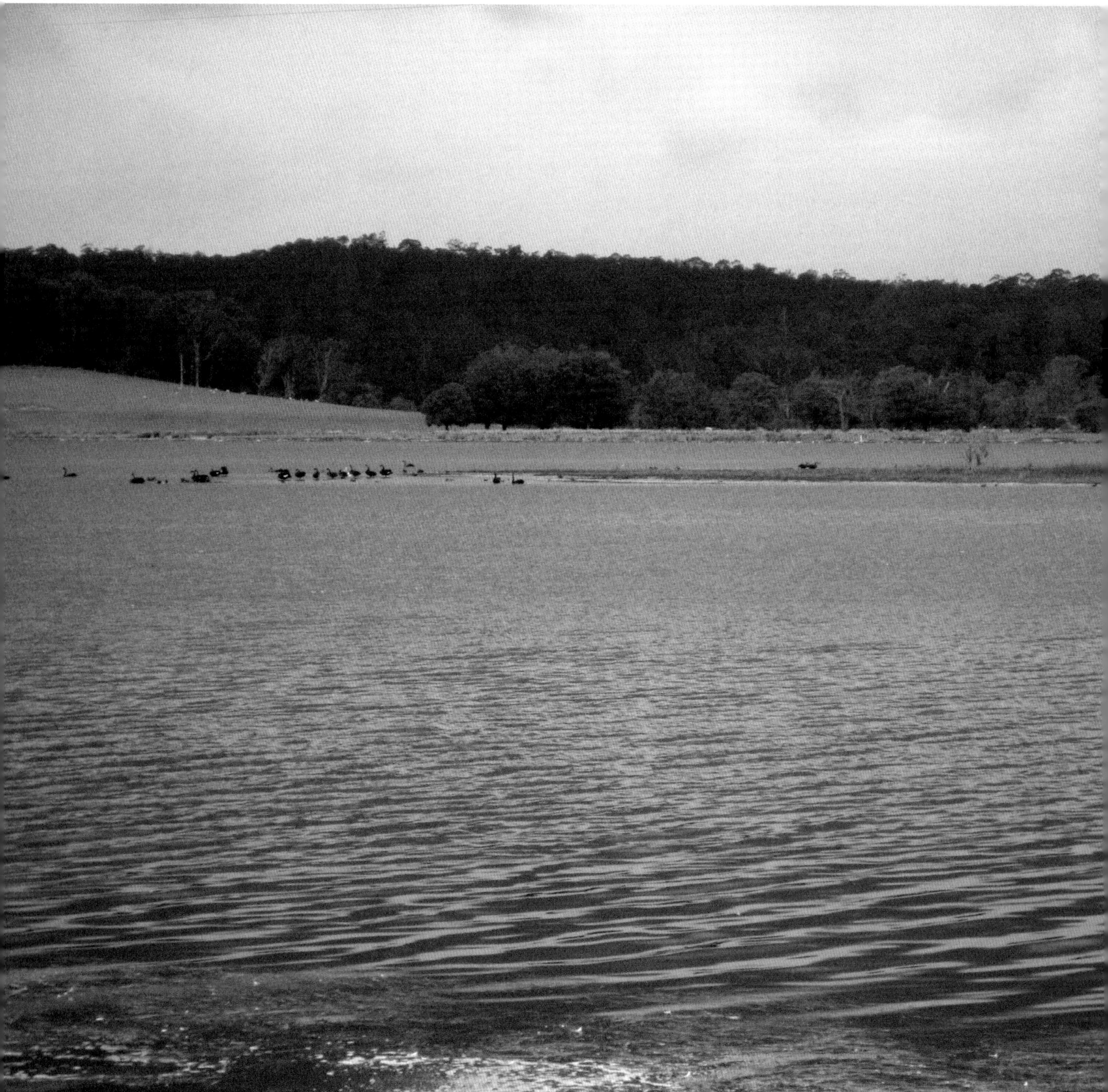

Ochres are a kind of clay and are used for many things, such as initiation ceremony or healing. There are different ochres for different purposes, but you have to know where to look for them and which ones you can eat, and which ones can be painted on the body.

There's the hard ochre that needs to be crushed from the rock. Where we look out over Barran-guba, along the coast on the cliff face, there are two streams of ochres, one red, the other white. The red ochre would go on the living family at a funeral and would indicate these people were still alive and had fresh blood. White ochre would be put on the person who had passed over to indicate that they had passed into the spirit world.

There's a type of white ochre that you put on the body when dancing. There is also another ochre that is found near water and is used to help trauma. The ochre usually has some little plants growing close by and the water would carry properties from these special plants to the ochre. I won't name these plants, but they used to be put on us if something traumatic happened. The wet ochre would be rubbed onto the forehead and some on the body. The people would say, 'This will stop you from going mad or insane.'

There's also some ochre for the woman that helps with morning sickness. When they are pregnant the women can suck on the ochre, as it is fine and smooth.

We use ochre when we go on Gulaga. When we first go up, we count how many people are going up, and we stop and clap the sticks for each person to warn the spirits that we are coming. We also clap to make sure that there's a safe passage, that nobody falls over or break their legs, or injure themselves. And nobody has done it yet. We come with respect; we wear the red headband and we put the three bits of ochre on our foreheads.

The middle dot lets us see what we're talking about. The other two dots are for opening up your minds, your two minds. There's a saying in English: 'You were in two minds'. These are your thinking mind and your coordinating mind. So you're going to need a coordinating mind to walk in sometimes and make decisions. There's a dot on the chin for the silence. Silence is for respect for the Elders that have left us the stories that I call legacies.

Page 123: Young men join the Doonooch Dancers at Woggan-ma-gule ceremony, 2009. Left: Wallaga Lake. This is a sacred lake because of all different kinds of seafood we could gather from here. We held ceremony around the foreshores of the lake and painted our bodies with ochre. Not just any rock could be an ochre. Ochres come from rocks found in special places, usually near water or plants with special healing properties. Ochre also indicated that fresh water was nearby, which was good if you lived near the sea. Ochres were used for decorating spears and paintings. They were also really good to use for cooking. You could plaster a fish or a game bird up in ochre and throw it on a fire. After a while you took it out, tapped on the clay to see if it was hard, then busted it open. The meat would be cooked and all the scales and feathers would have disappeared and the bellies shrivelled into a little ball, so there was no need to clean the animal before cooking it.

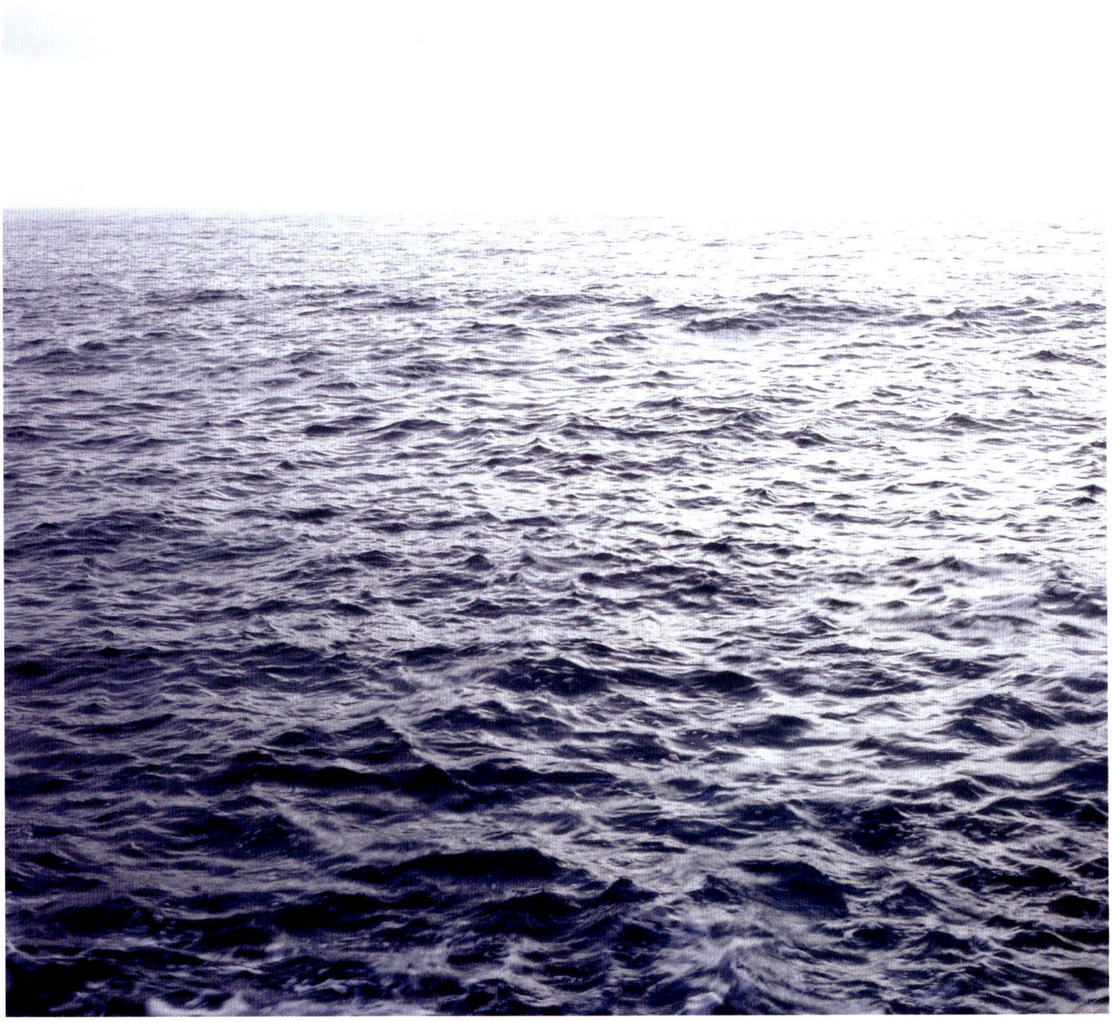

WHALE ELDERS

"Whales used to be Elders on the land, flesh Elders, but then they moved to the sea to protect the fish and look after the food and medicines there."

Gurawill the whale comes and beaches itself on our shores. I have three ancient spears that have been passed on to me: one is for spearing fish, another for hand-to-hand combat. The other spear is made from a hard sturdy wood and is for Gurawill.

Most of the whales and fish were once Elders on the land but now they are the Elders of the sea. Each and every one of them would have to hold the same Law of the sea. There is a time for them to come back in, a matter of them giving up their lives. Imagine a beautiful beach that you're standing upon and looking along its shores. Imagine one of those great mammals coming into the shore. Hearing the noise they make, communicating with some of the Elders on the shores, who would say 'We got Gurawill coming in now to regurgitate his lore'.

It's a strange way to describe what would take place but that's what Gurawill would do. As they would be approaching the channels and coming into the beaches, some of the men would get their great spears, these long, hard thick spears that were carved from hardwood trees, and drive them into Gurawill. Then they would lean against the spear and tilt it, so the whale would start to roll over. The rest of the men would pull the whale over and put him belly up, facing the heavens. This would allow the spirit of the whale to leave the body.

Then the message would get out and all the different clans and mobs would arrive to feast on the whale that had given up his life so that law could be known. While the people were eating the flesh of the whale they would be learning more of the wisdom of the ocean and the land and sharing and caring with each other of what they were feasting on, passing laws on to other clan groups.

Sometimes the whale would come in numbers, but usually the solitary one was the one that brought the Law of the sea.

Kyandle sitting in the whale rock on Barran-guba. Whales have been beaching themselves long before modern day technology got here and interfered with the natural wiring of Earth, way back before radar, pollution, all those theories. This practice goes back thousands of years. The old people say the whale comes in to give its life so that they can share the lore. Through eating the flesh of the whale they were being given permission to talk about the lore.

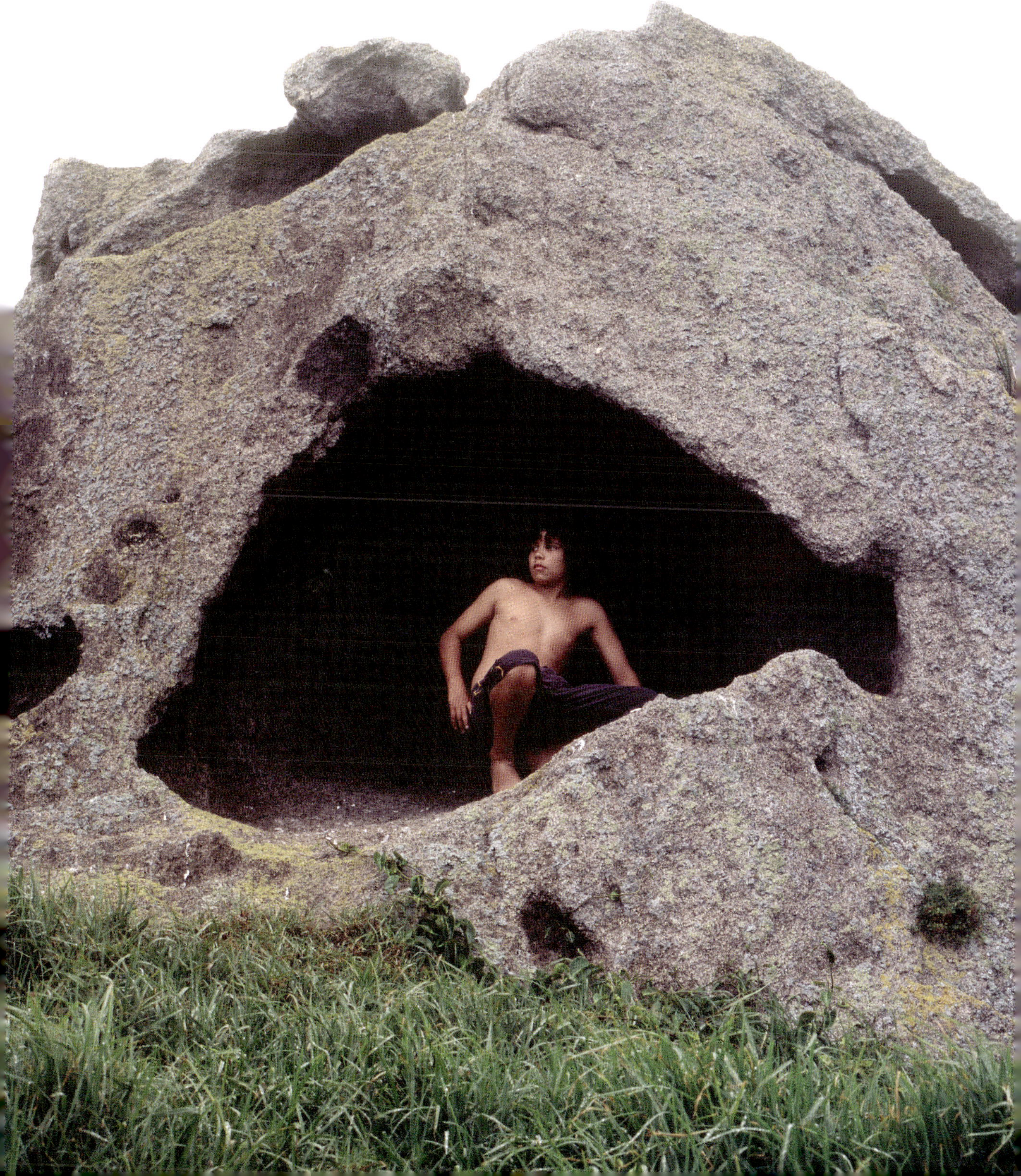

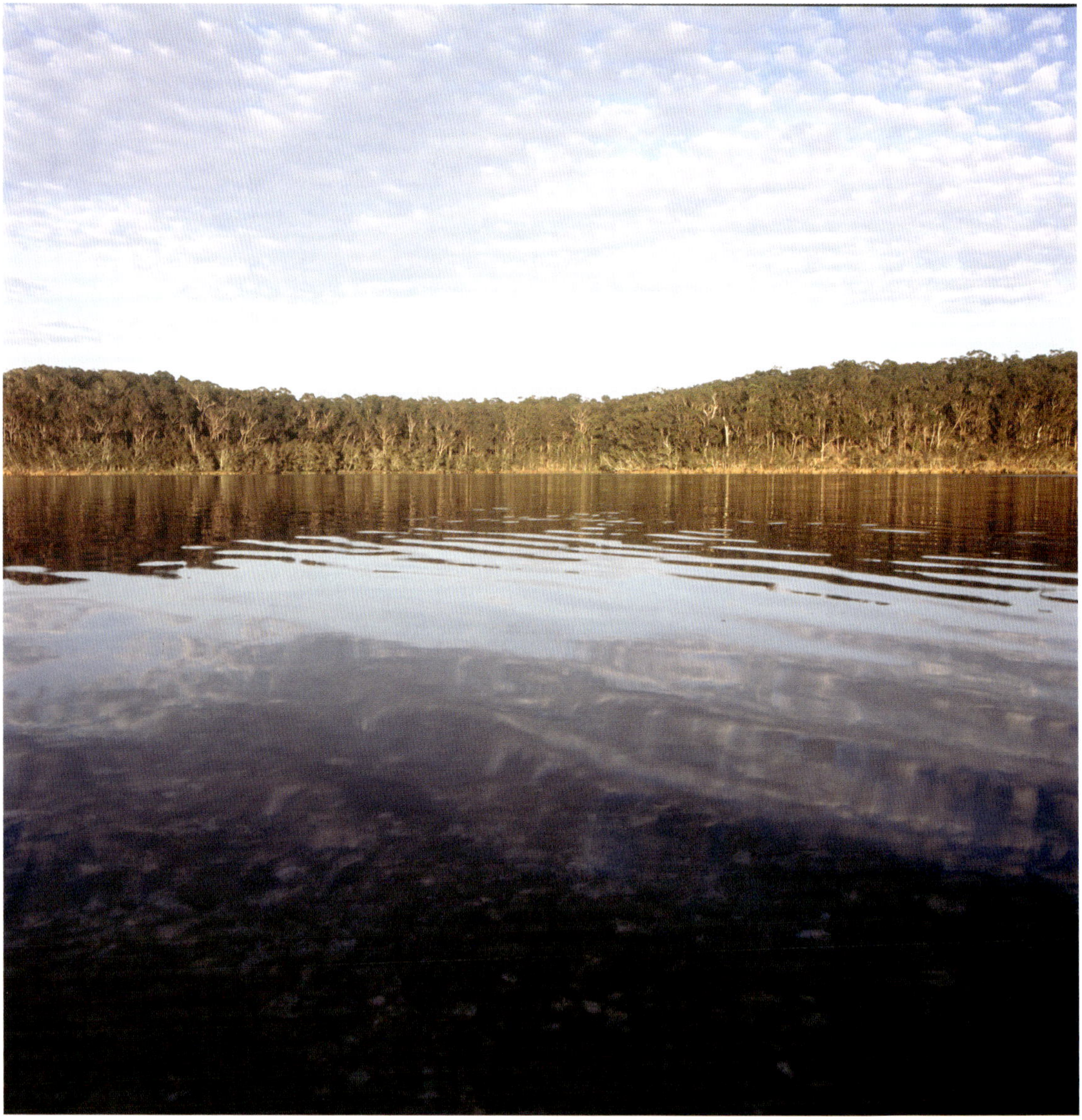

Boundaries and Borders

"*Some people think language is just talking, here and there, but it is much more. It represents a border and it holds culture and law.*"

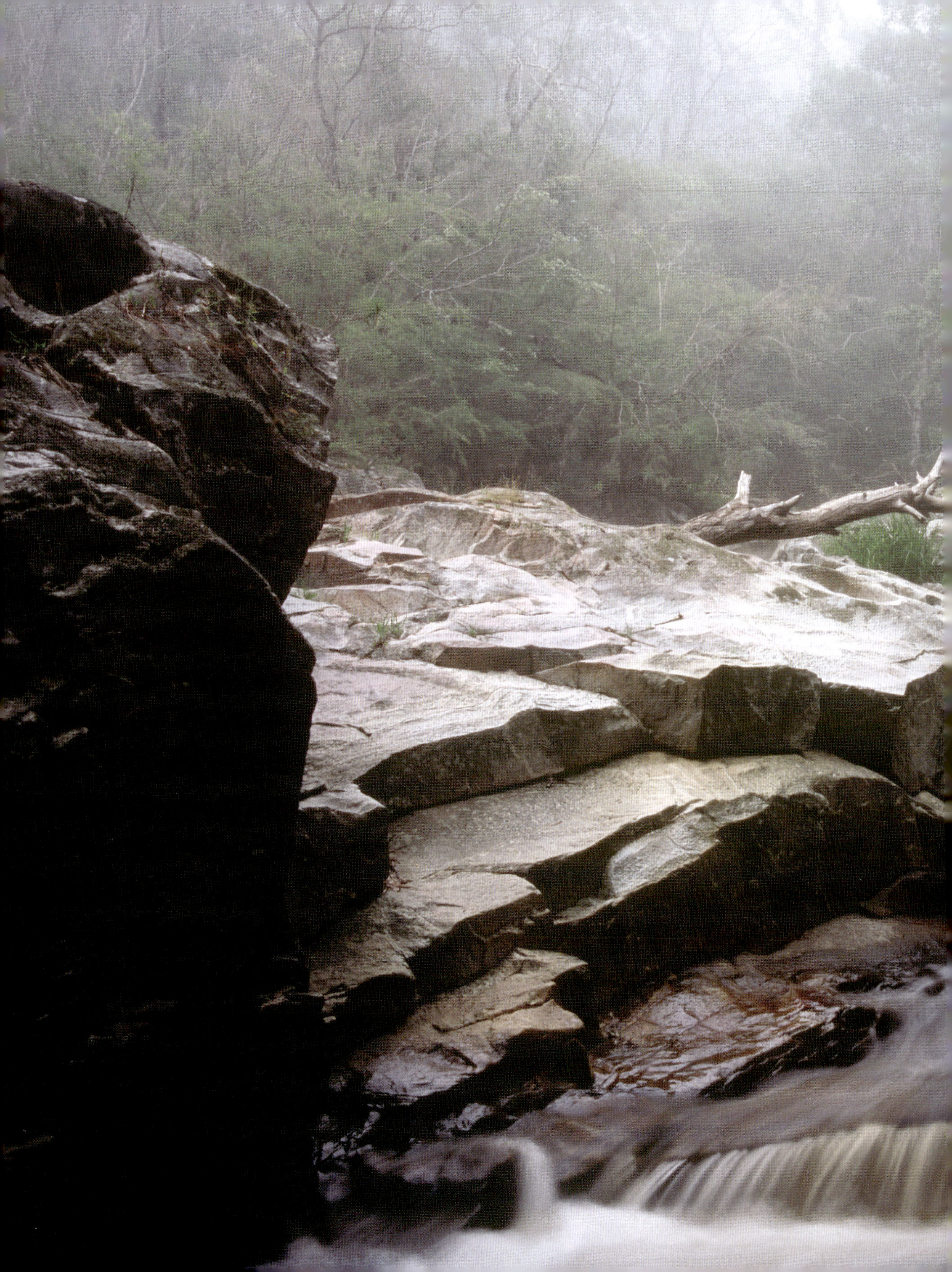

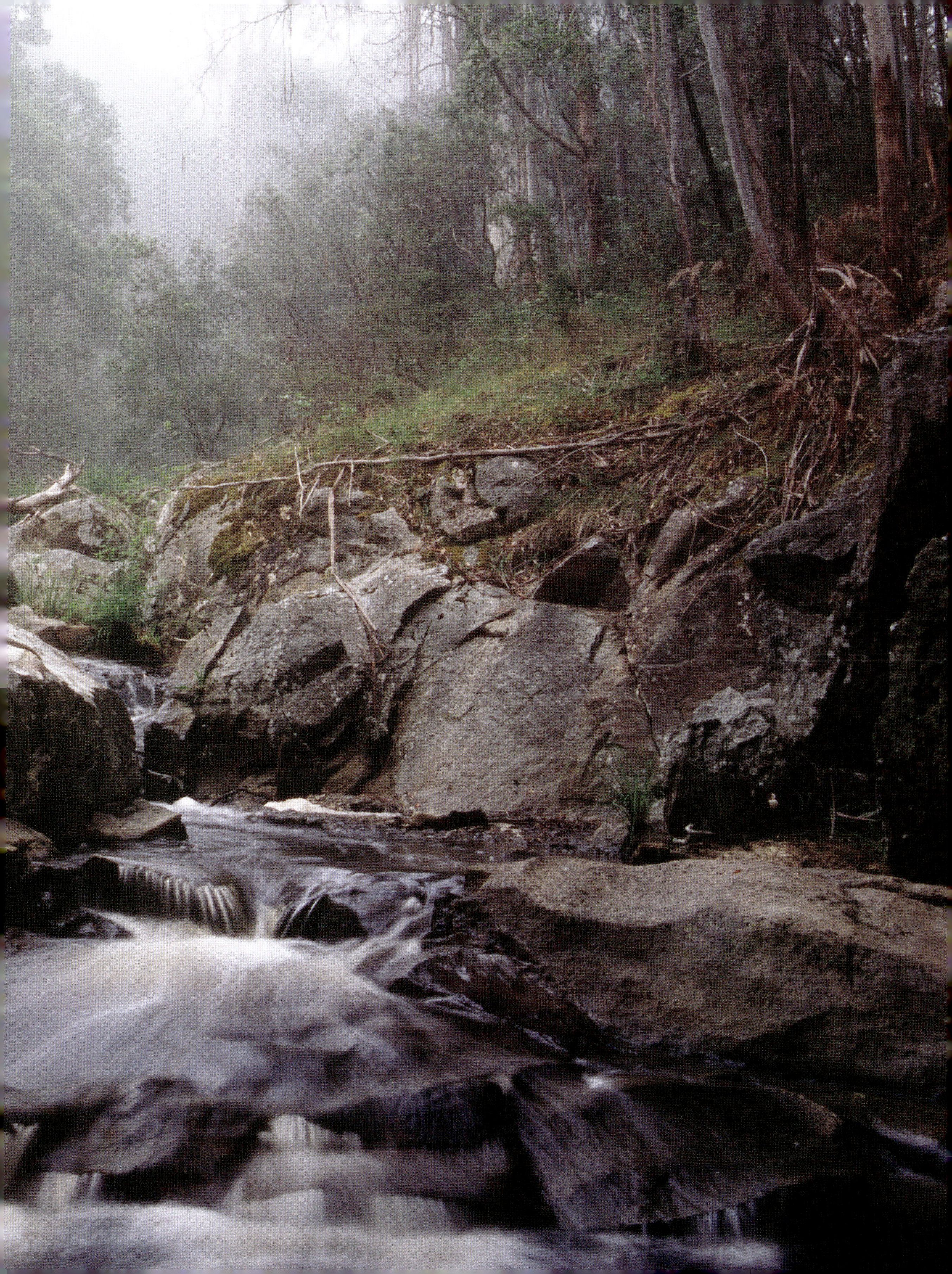

Tribal boundaries or borders are a way of life in the Aboriginal communities. People with nomadic lifestyles knew how important it was to maintain and keep each and every one of them. They didn't go uninvited across the boundaries without permission. The only time tribal warfare would break out was when the young men would be too eager in their hunting. If they moved into a territory where they were not supposed to be, that is when warfare would break out.

There are also borders between the tribes and the aquatic people [*dolphins*] in the animal world. There's always a border there. The simple thing is you don't step over the line, because you put yourself in danger, no matter what.

The borders and territories of water, the territories of going around rocks and what you have to confront there, the wobegong, the shark or the stingray, have to be approached with caution and with respect. Everything was done respectfully by the tribes. They had to practise the laws at all times and not go up against them and try to break those rules, you see.

There's also borders and boundaries in storytelling; there's boundaries in languages. We can't take one language inland from the coast because you're taking it out of its homeland, you're bringing it out of its sacredness. It is such an important thing to watch your boundaries, your creeks, your rivers and mountains. Holding language is another wonderful way of looking after your boundaries. Some people think language is just talking, here and there, but its much more. It represents a border and it holds culture and law.

Previous page: If we read the signs nature shows us where our boundaries are; the slipperiness of the rocks tell us to be careful and not tread there. Right: Spotted gums at Mystery Bay. Boundaries were kept even on the coastal strips on the ocean where people would gather shellfish. They would look at the leftover shells on the middens (pile of shells) to see which type of shellfish had been eaten by the mob that went before them or had a ceremony before them. By seeing the leftover shells people knew they were the ones they shouldn't eat, and those borders within borders were respected.

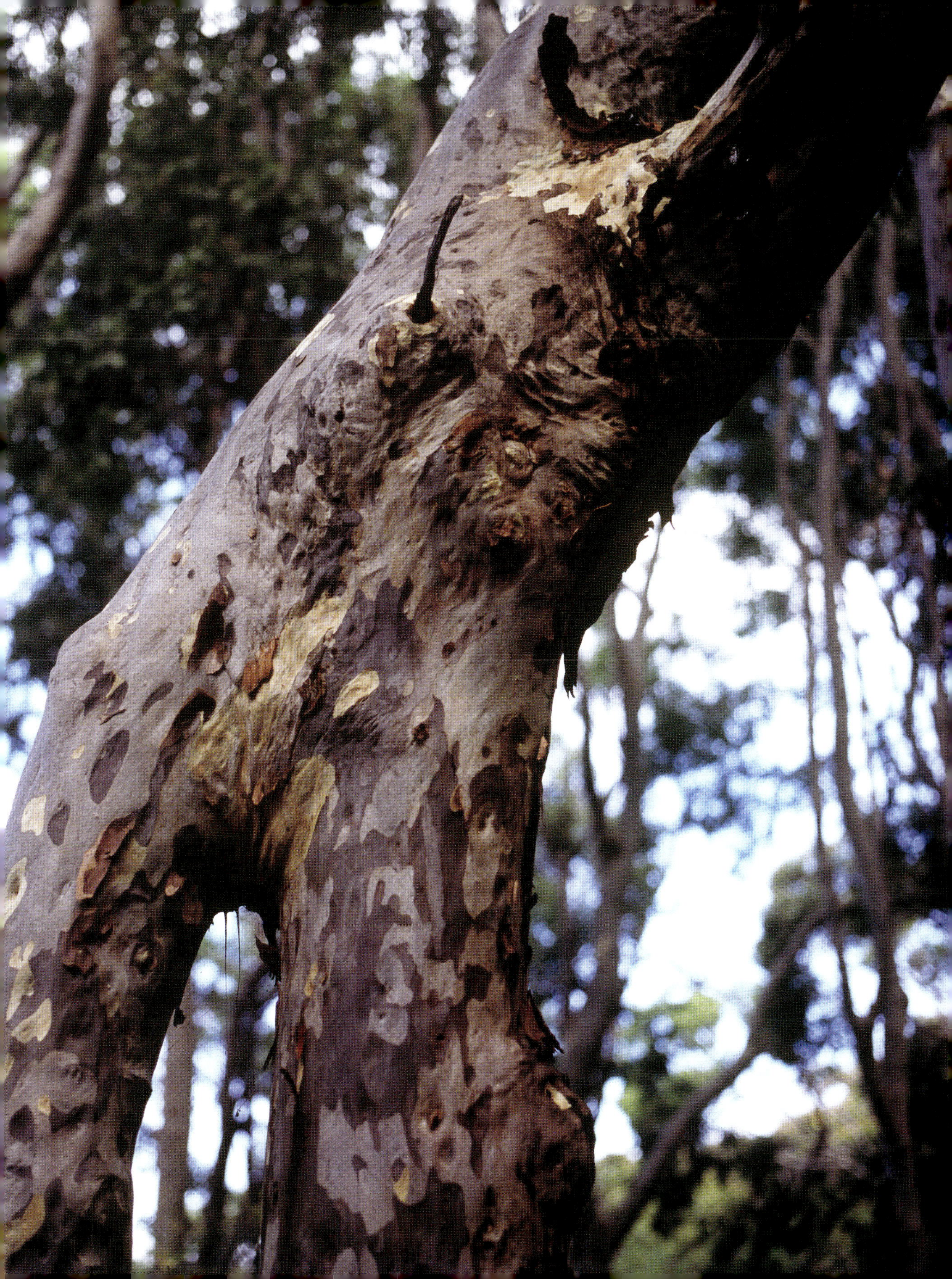

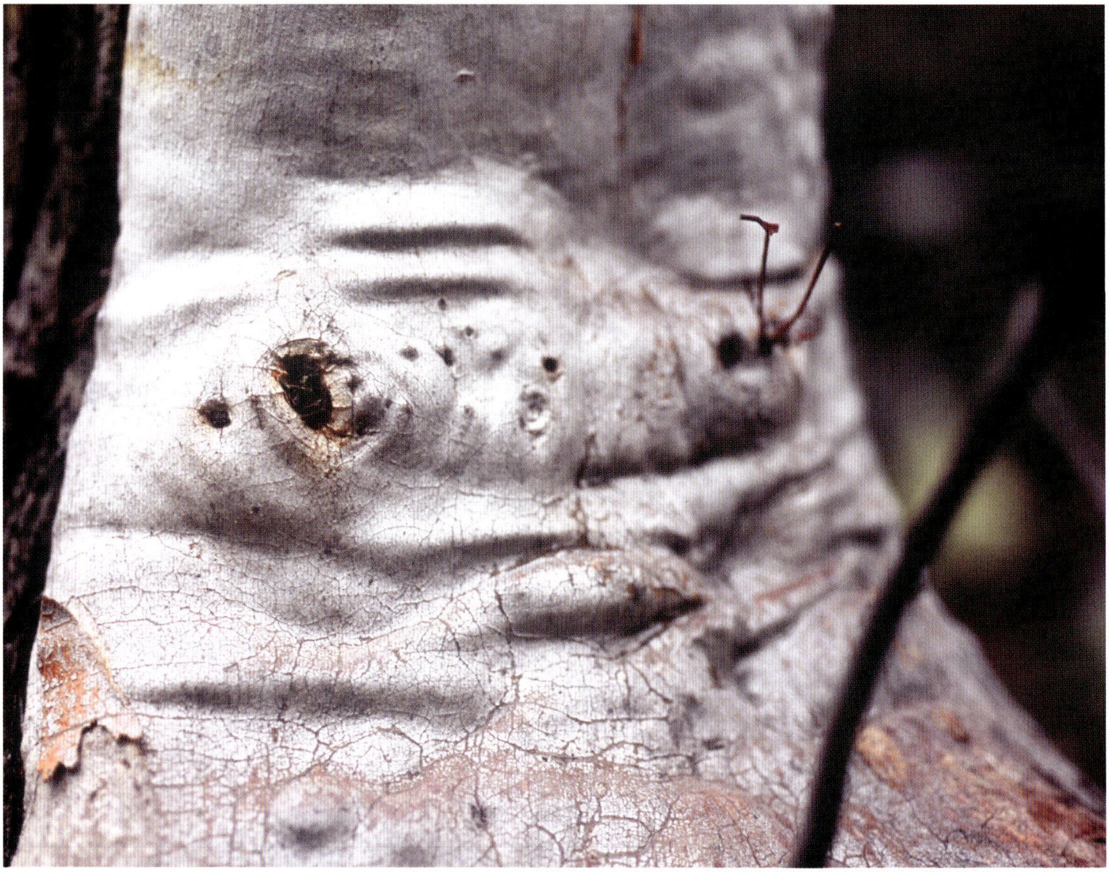

SINGING TREE

"Trees live in tribes, just like people. When a tree is born and then it is moved to another area for whatever reason, that's like taking a person out of their country and putting them in a different country. They become like refugees."

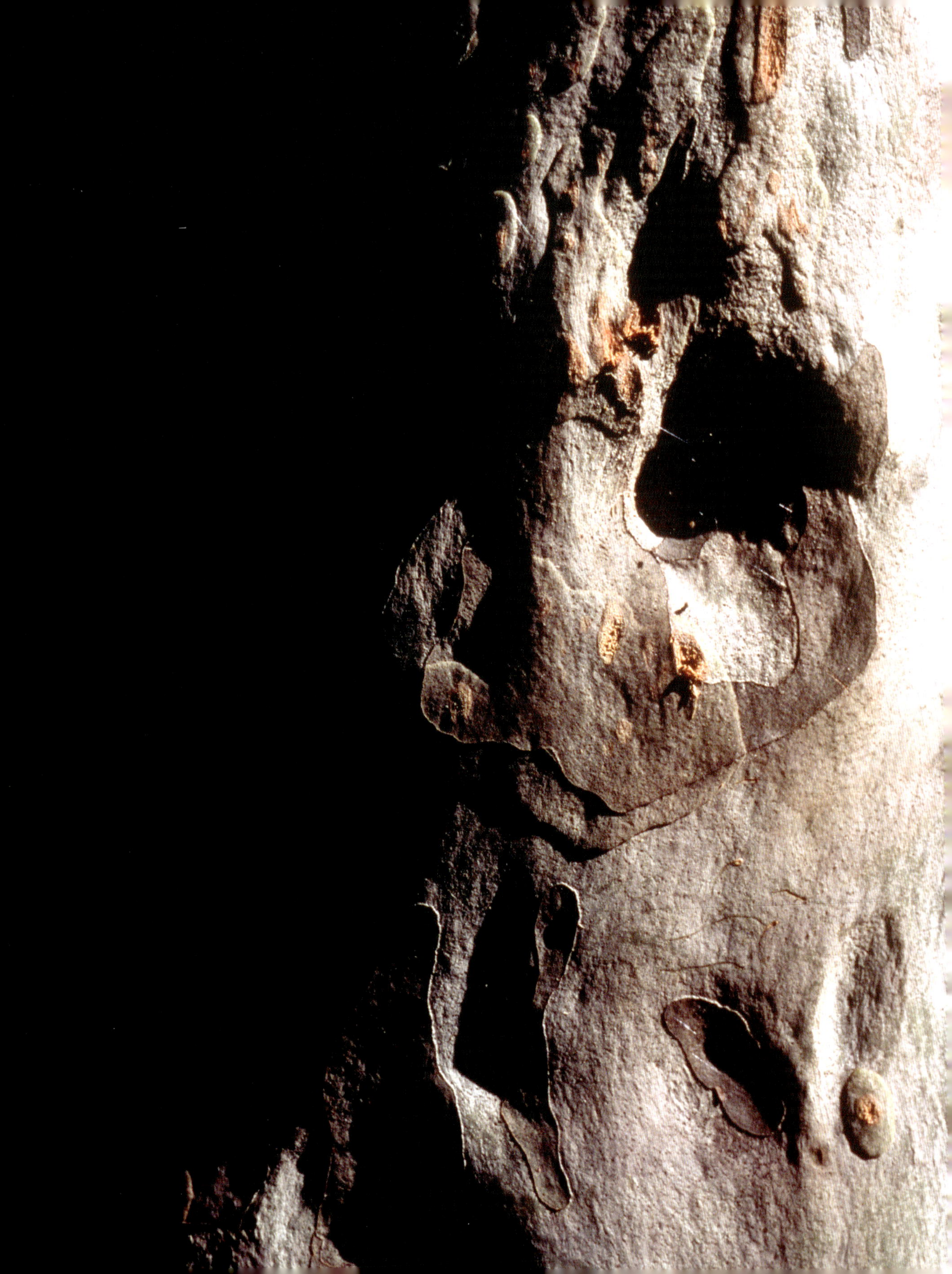

Put your ear against a young tree and give it a gentle shake. Listen to its song being sung. You can hear the sound travelling, it travels down into the roots. It's telling the roots to hang on, we're shaking up here in the breeze. If your eyes could show you all of the tree, you could see those roots hanging on. That tree is recording everything from its leaves to its roots and all around it that passes through it and connects with it. I don't think people would hurt the trees if they heard its song. Trees tell us about the health of our environment. We look to trees to tell us how the world is coping.

We call the banksia trees 'the Elder trees'. Trees with smooth trunks are female, while the big old rough trees are male trees. Angophoras, they are old female trees. If you look at a tribe of angophoras that's sprouted out from some rocks you will see they are so huge and how they twist and turn and are embracing everything. Once you start looking at those old grannies, as we call them, then you know 'Whoa, there's a women's place somewhere round about here,' because they are used as a signpost. When you look at those old grannies, they are nurturing and they are holding things, you have got all those kind of limbs twisting and turning, you see what grannies and mothers do. That's how you identify them like that.

All trees live in tribes, just like people. When a tree is born and then it's moved to another area for whatever reason, that's like taking a person out of their country and putting them in a different country.

A face in the tree ... can you see the spirit?

Tree planting needs a ceremony, especially if you move a tree from its tribe to another tribe. You can move the tree but you do ceremony as well. You do ceremony because the precious life of that tree has got to be really cared for, not just watered and put things around it, but it's got to be sung into the land. It must always be sung into the land, and proper ceremony done so there's still a sacred connectedness. That's very important for tree planting. Not just plant them willy-nilly. It's like refugees today. Have a look at them. Have a look at the poor people today, all they have done is come here out of wars, and they are being dumped in cities. If you look at the Sudanese, they are trying to teach them to work in offices when they are farmers. They have been displaced.

Can you see how this tree and rock are working in partnership to live together? The rock is telling the roots of the tree, 'Hey, you can come down here, and you can come down there and I will support you.' This is how we work with the land, supporting and helping each other.

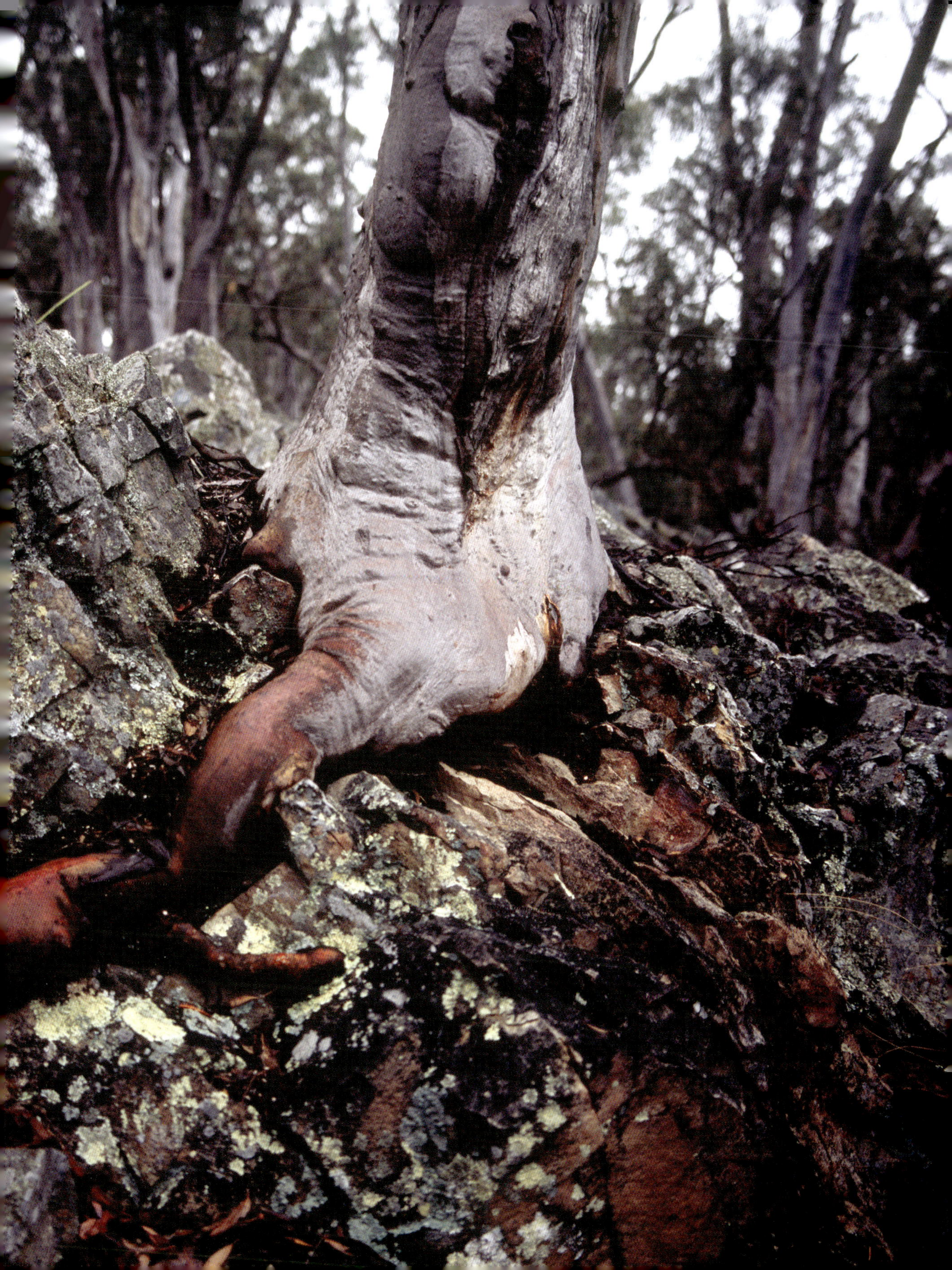

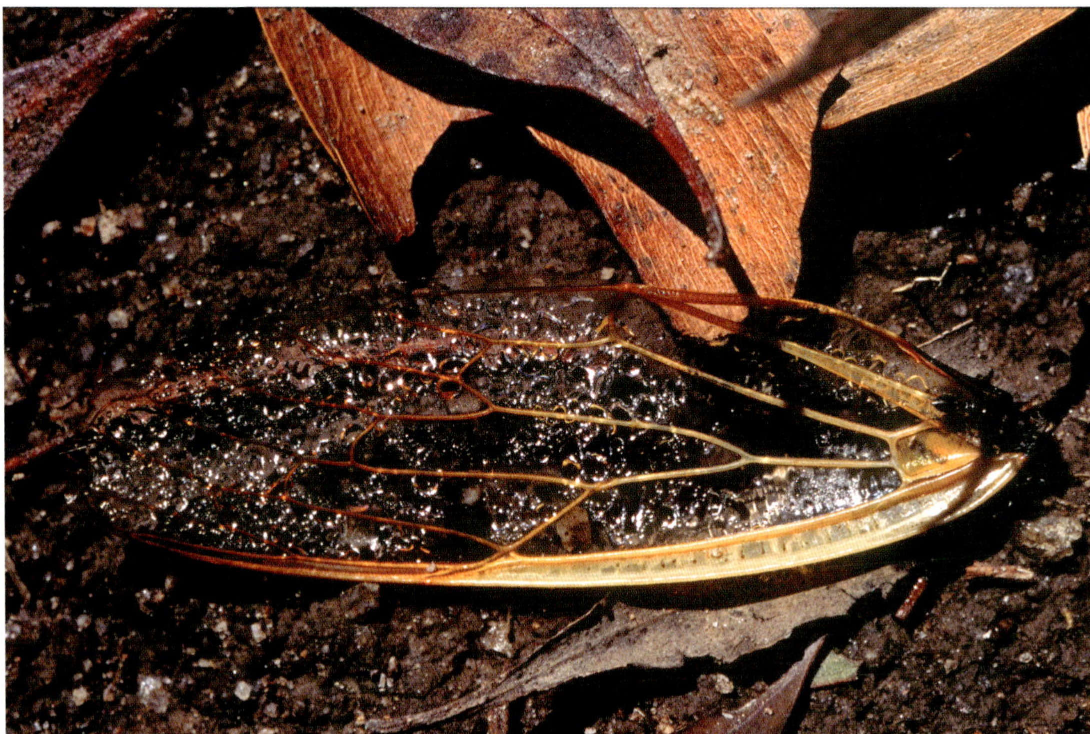

FOOD AS MEDICINE

"Not only can we use the food around us to heal ourselves but we can also use it to heal the environment or ask for help from the environment. The seaweed is part of our rain-making ceremony. We would collect a bit of that and throw it on a fire near the beach and get a good bit of rain."

You can work with food and heal with it; it's medicine. It's designed to maintain health. These days you can pay for a plate of food. It's put together on that plate to look and taste great. It will fill your belly, but the life force in it, that healing quality, is long gone by the time it's put in front of you.

If you want to be healthy then respect your body by what you put into it. Respect is the important thing on all levels. In life it precedes the action, it keeps those spiritual doors open so you can move forward and not get stuck.

The diet of the Aboriginal people from birth was mother's milk. As the babies began to grow, it would change to yams, berries, different fruits, fish and snakes – whatever was gathered and hunted for them.

The easy access to the tucker was stopped when settlers started to spread out across the land, and built the fences and developed private property. The easy access to the natural foods became hard to get. Our people would be charged, flogged or shot for looking for food in the traditional way.

In the early to late 1800s and into the 1900s, the government were putting people onto the missions, herding us like cattle. They could see the Koori's physiques were slender and muscular from natural diets and exercise from walking and hunting and gathering, but they looked on us as underfed and malnourished. The good Christians, in what they thought was wisdom, looked at these skinny blackfellas and said, 'We better cover them up and put clothes on them and feed them proper food.' And that's when the sugars and flours and other foods came into our diet. The metabolism of our bodies couldn't take this food, that's when diabetes and overweight body shapes occurred, and as a consequence we weren't in shape to hunt or gather. We became disconnected from the Earth Mother for nutrition, and dependent on the white man's tucker.

This seaweed is part of our rain-making ceremony. We would burn it on a fire and ask for rain... and it would come.

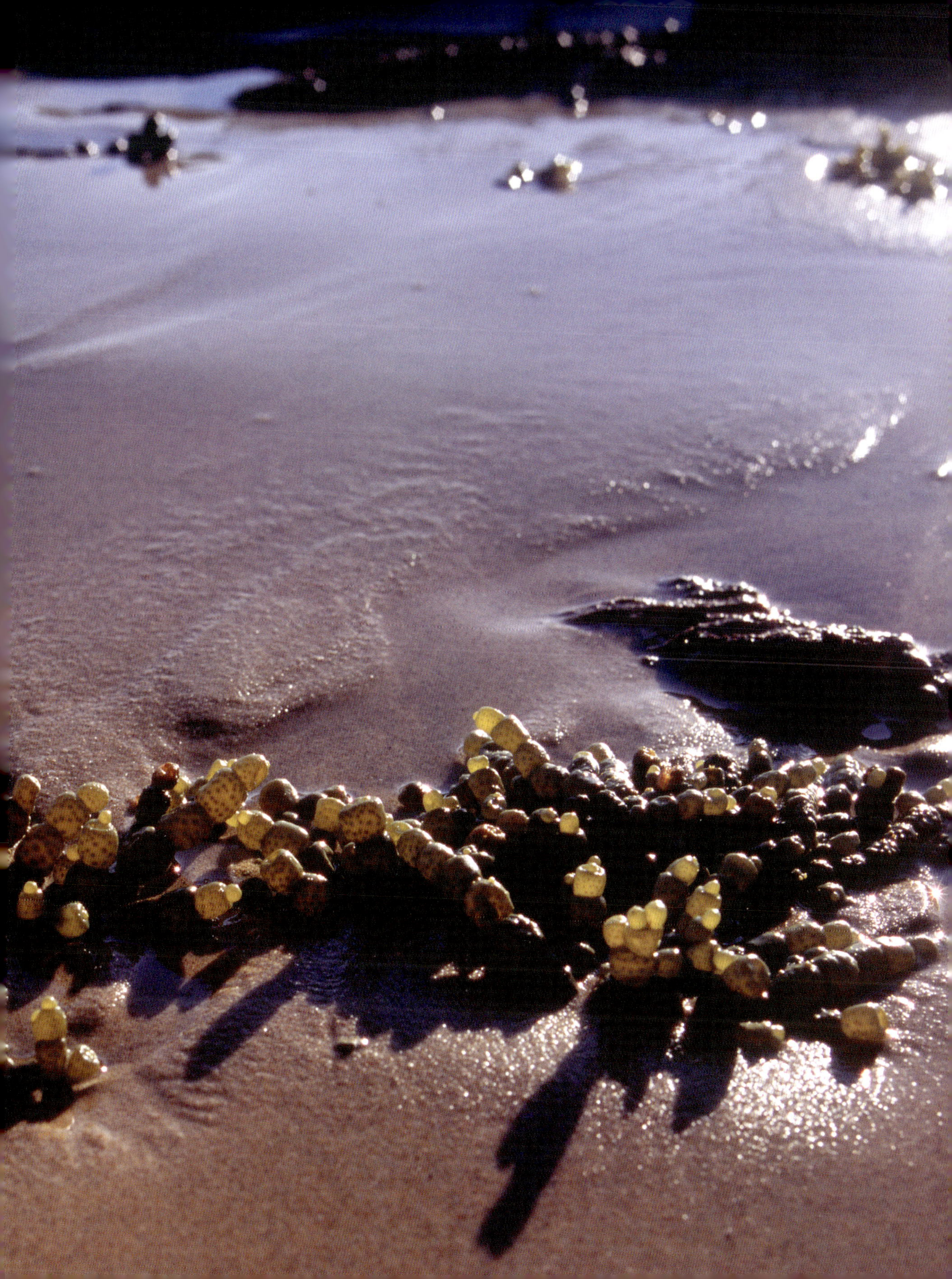

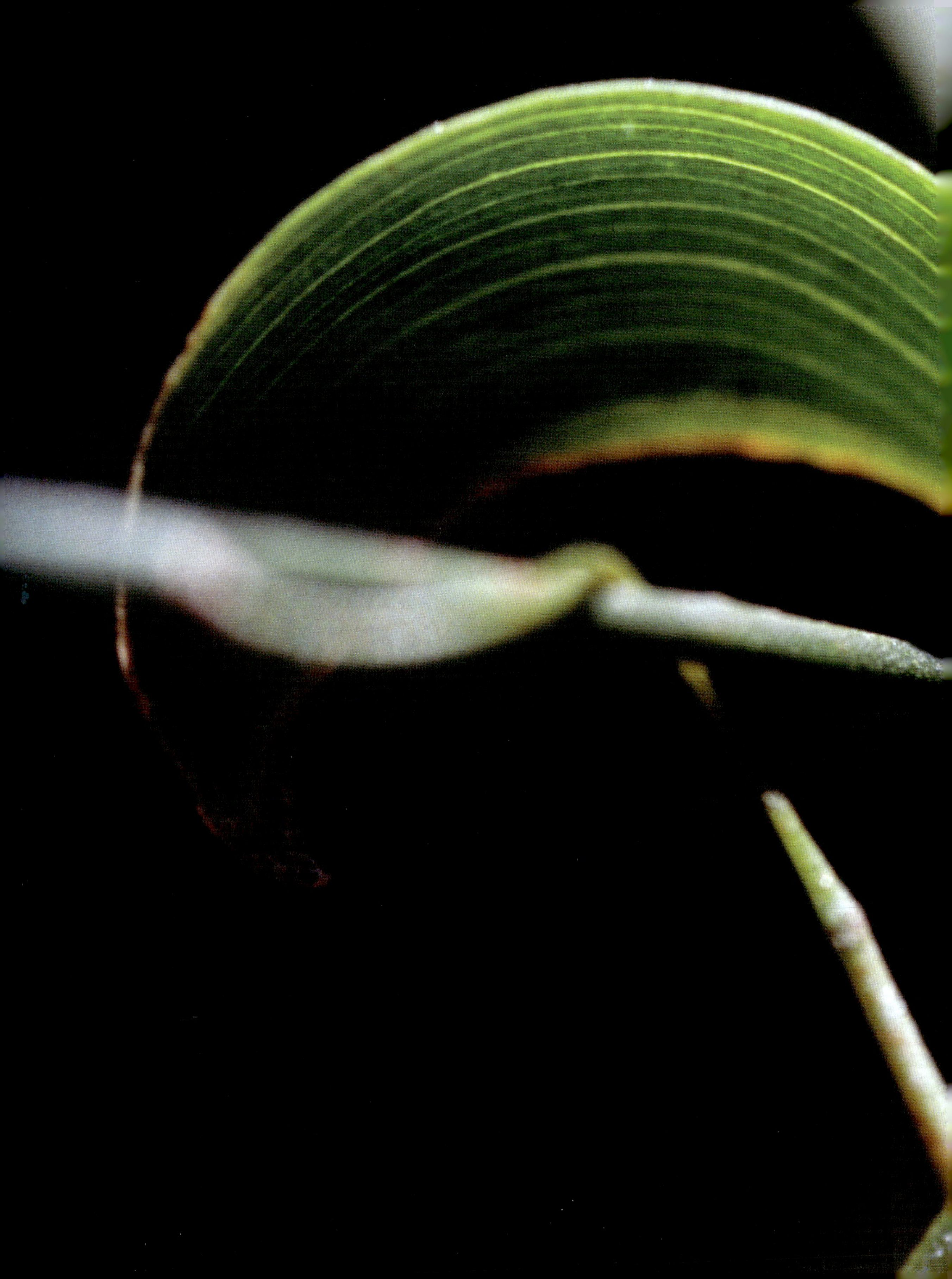

So the Christians clothed us and fattened us up, and the ironic thing that I see is no-one wants to be fat now; they found out about disease that comes through being overweight. Now people are paying to get slim, taut and terrific and yet our people were already doing that, as every time we had a feed we walked from point A to point B. It was a natural thing for us to do. We always exercised, it was how we got around and found our food. No need for a gym, the land gives us our shape.

The minute the Christians started to put clothes, coats and blankets around our naked bodies that's when our immune system went down. It was devastating to our people. They had lost their immunity, their strong natural ability to ward off sickness. That is why our mob has the worst health in Australia today, our immune systems have changed and broken down, coughs and colds have become deadly to us.

Our bodies were used to the nakedness, used to the cold, and every time we swam in Gadu we would ingest salt down the throat and nose, and that salt would help build up immunity against our winter ailments. So if you're feeling a little unwell the best thing you can do is jump into the ocean, no matter how cold or whatever – that helps fight off sickness.

The only thing our people had wrapped around them in the extreme cold was kangaroo or possum cape, just thrown around us or thrown over us when we were sleeping.

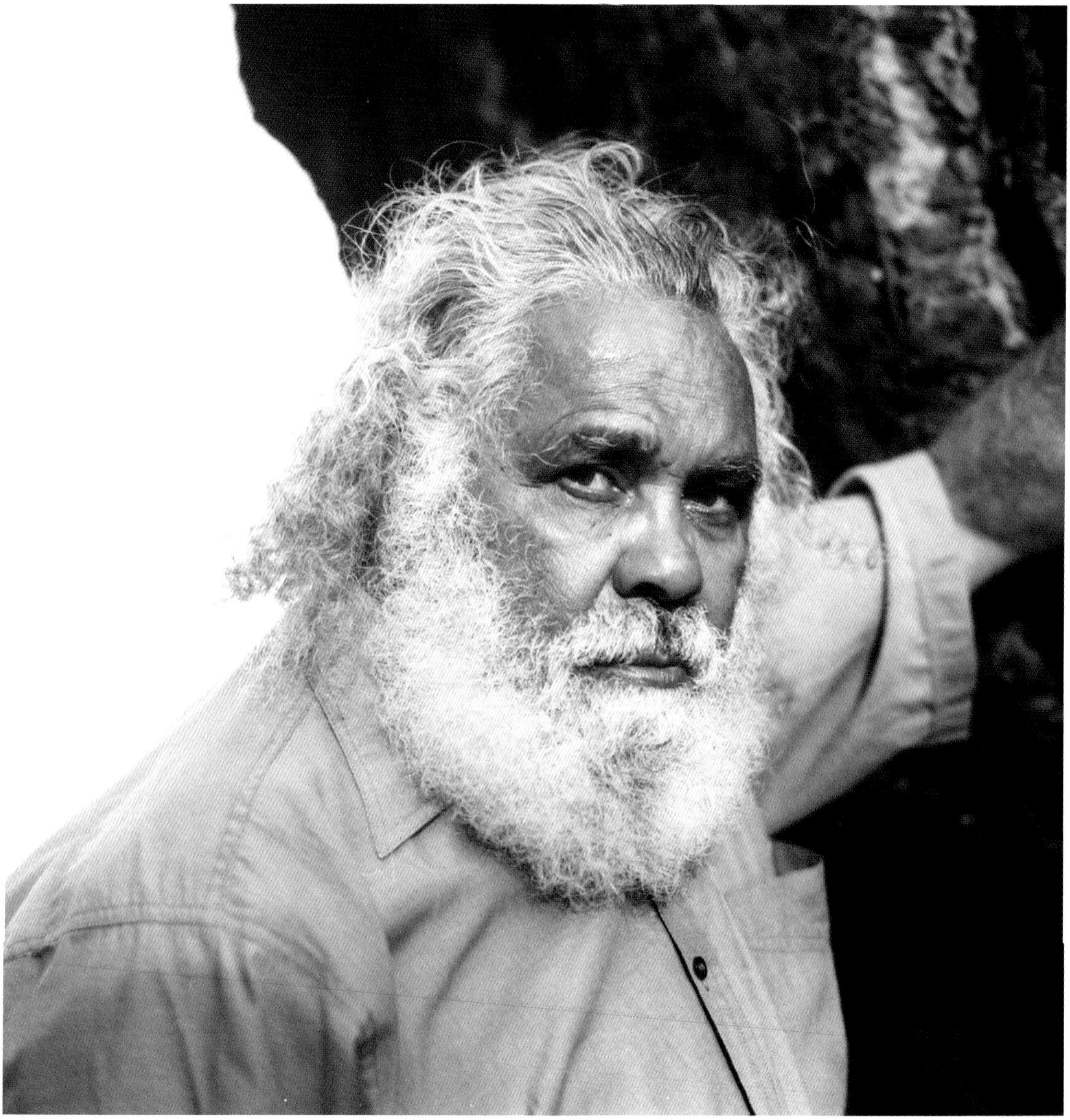

FORGIVENESS

"*It's a pretty big call to forgive ... Forgiveness is for your healing. It's your self-healing, it's got nothing to do with the person that has probably done wrong.*"

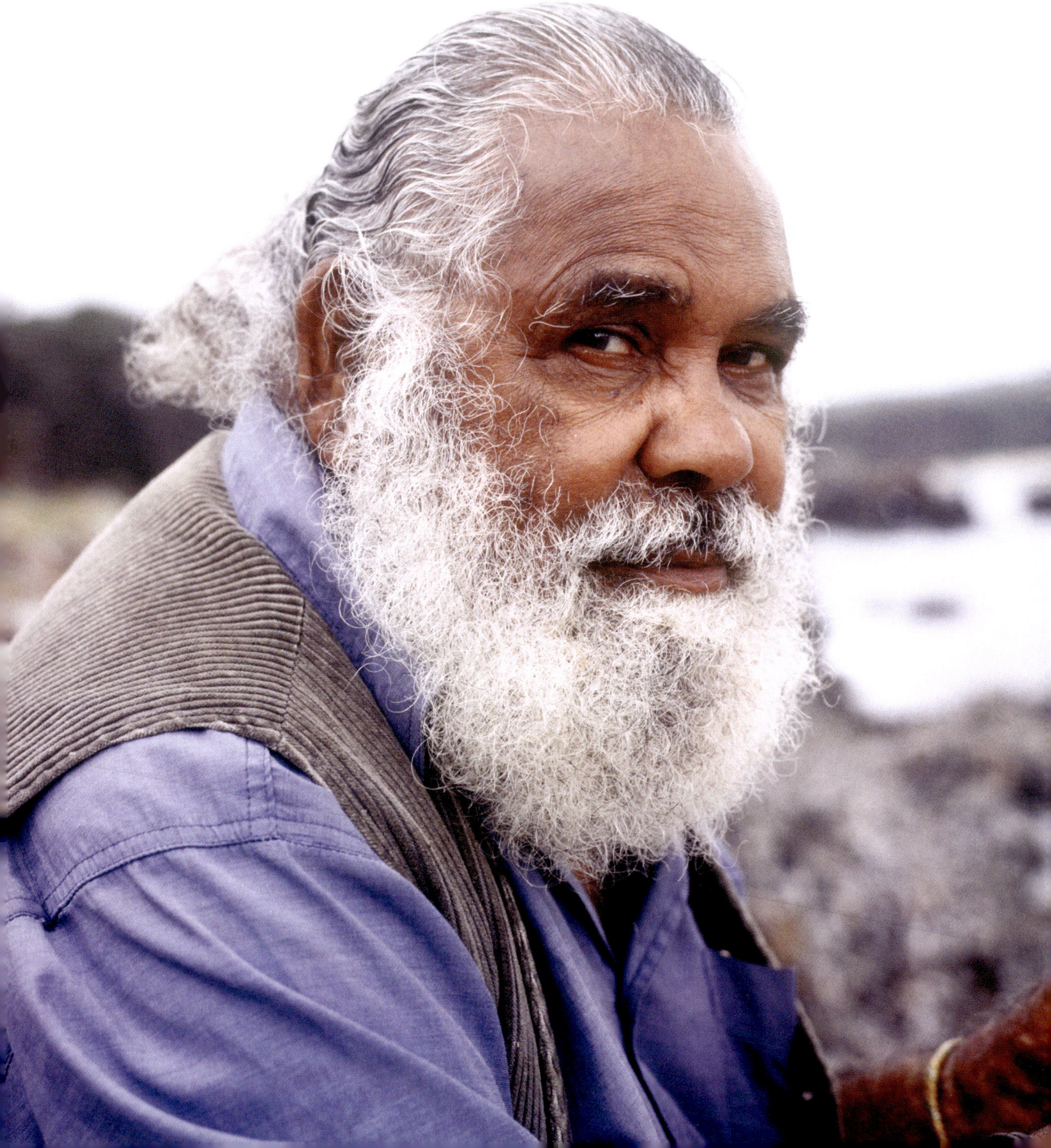

It's a pretty big call to forgive. Forgiveness is one of the extreme points of spirituality and personal growth. Forgiveness can happen on a small scale and on a big scale too.

I remember the phone call I got back in 2000 and it was my sister-in-law down in the state of Victoria. I can hear her crying and I said, 'What's up, Sis?' She said 'Oh Brother, it's Tony …' and Tony is my son, my eldest son. Now our mob, when someone does something wrong or mucks up, we say, 'What's the mongrel done?' and we mean it in a kind of loving way. So I said, 'Okay, what did the mongrel do now? Did he muck up and do something?' She said 'No, Brother, he hung himself.' When she said that, well, I couldn't say anything. I still had the phone up to my ear. And she said, 'Did you hear what I said, Brother?' Through her sobs I said, 'Yes, Sis. I heard what you said. Anthony hung himself.' Then because I can hear the pain of my sister-in-law on the other end of the phone, I said, 'Son, I forgive you.' It was as simple as that. I said, 'I forgive you, Son, and I love you.' What I meant by that was I forgave him for the pain that he was causing the family when the rest of the news spread around, through Victoria and all around New South Wales.

This is taken near Mystery Bay. The beaches behind me were used for burial grounds because it was easier to dig in the sand.

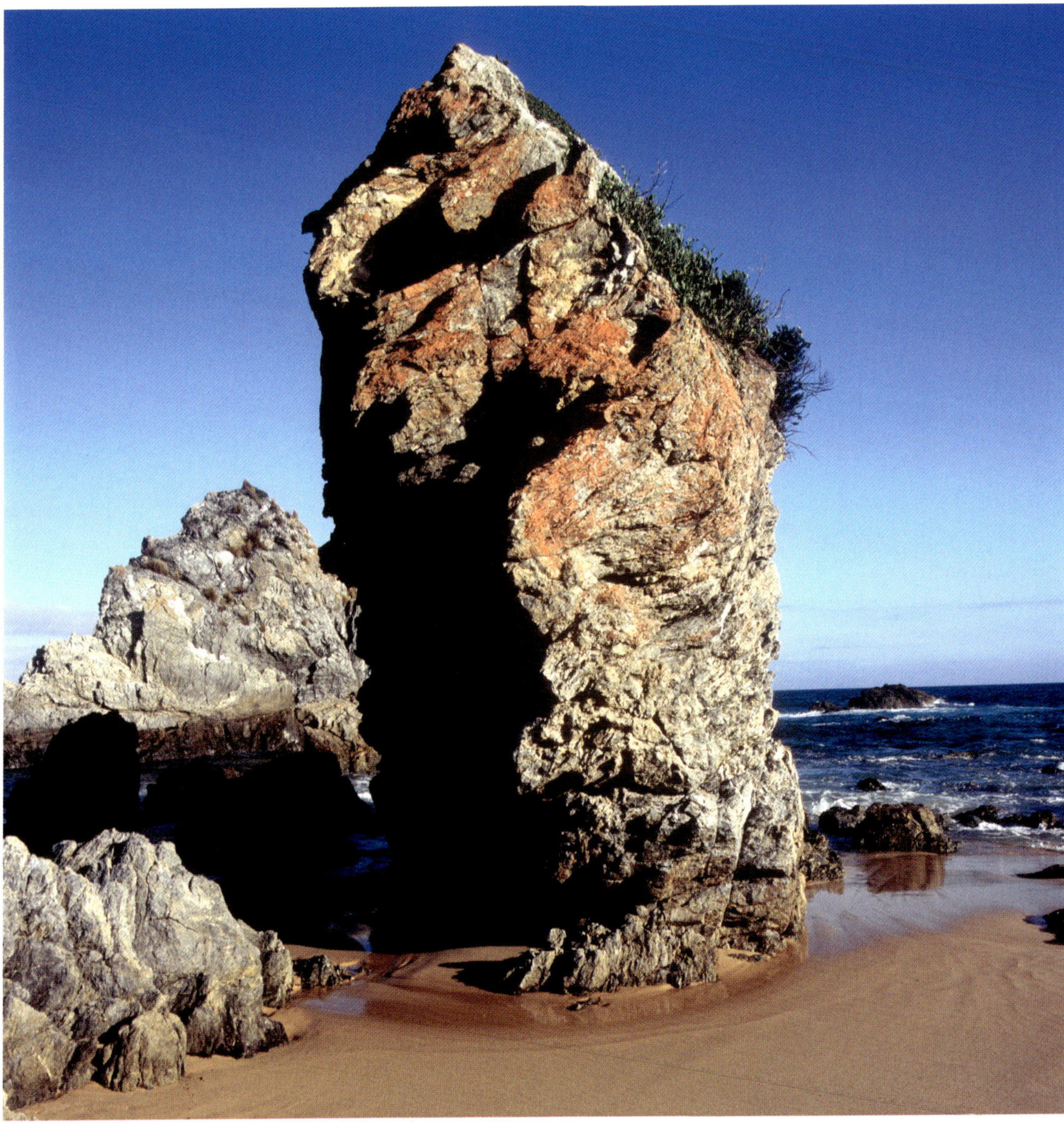

I forgave him for the pain that he caused his mother and his father and his brothers and sisters. I forgave him for the pain that he caused his two children and grandchild. I forgave him for the pain that he caused all his cousins and mates who loved him. It was easier then for me to forgive him for what he had done, instead of asking a silly question that's got no answer to it such as, 'Why?' 'Why did you do this, Son? What happened?' It would be senseless asking all those silly questions, doing a post mortem then, when he wasn't even two hours cold, or two hours in death. I knew that I would have to forgive my son for the pain that he had caused families.

To do that I had to do some self-healing first. My mind headed down to Gulaga, down to the three rocks that sit on top of one another. I went to the middle rock, the one that lets you do your own personal inventory and helps in a crisis. In that instant I was there, I looked at where my son was heading, and where he came from.

And then I looked up from where he came from, and there was more coming up, there were his children, and his little grandchildren. And my great-grandchildren.

So I had to zip down there in that split second to get that forgiveness, and that's why I forgave him. Just visualising that part of the mountain, visualising that particular rock was a healing, was an instant healing for me.

Then I took this idea of forgiveness a step further when I was asked later after the year 2000: 'Uncle Max, what do you think of invasion?' I thought about that for a minute and I said, 'Well, it's not a great thing to invade other people's homeland and properties.' But then I began to really think about the concept of invasion and, in particular, the invasion into the eastern seaboard of this country. It made me really look at all the changes that have been forced upon us.

Kevin Rudds' apology to the Aboriginal people in 2008 really emphasised the stolen generations, but I had already forgiven all the past things. It wasn't just our children that was so forcibly removed, but a lot of our laws and practices, a lot of our languages and a lot of other things that were forcibly removed.

I see beauty in this rock, just as much beauty as there is in the rugged coastlines or in the green leafy bushes. The colour of the sky, the brown red of the rock... if someone was to destroy this rock they wouldn't destroy the memory of its spirit in me. Some people can't see the beauty of this rock and for that I forgive them. We all have different views on beauty.

Not everyone can forgive. Some people are very angry, some people are not moving and they will stay in sorrow times – have sorry days and that. I try not to get involved in those events of sorry days, because I don't want to be stuck in that energy of being sorry and not moving on. I want to keep surviving so that I can still embrace a lot of our culture and a lot of our knowledge – to help turn people around and say, 'Okay, this is what you are missing. Look at those plants and see what nature teaches you. This is how our lifestyle was; it wasn't in the suit, driving the Holden or the Ford Dreaming. It wasn't the Dollar Dreaming. It's nothing to do with that, you know. It was all about the land and what it can really, really give us.'

I think my ability to forgive I learned from my Uncles. Maybe the people that can't forgive didn't have examples like that to follow. I guess that could be it. Somewhere we are not given that knowledge of acceptance. I have been taught acceptance. You know, if you can practise the Law of acceptance in your life, then you can just about walk through most things in life, you see. That's where your forgiveness can be the front-runner there.

There might be the idea that being able to accept things means I don't stand up for myself.

But I don't want that language tarnishing my spirituality, you know. I am here. I woke up this morning. I see that first little bit of light, and I have to accept that is the first day for the rest of my life. That is so important. Tomorrow is not here, but just that first little bit of light that I can see when I wake up in the morning is my acceptance and knowing: 'Today I am alive, I am going to get up in a minute, it's going to be cold. I can feel that, so I know I am alive. I am going to get up and make a cup of tea. I know I am alive.' These are things that have been taught to me and I put into practice.

Forgiveness is for your healing. It's your self-healing, it's got nothing to do with the person that has probably done wrong. If you want to breathe that cancer within your spirit, then you are the one that will get sick.

So, forgiveness is such an important part of your recovery. It is one of the highest extreme levels of acceptance. It's one of the greatest achievements if you can forgive – your spirit stays free. It's not caught up in that turmoil of anger and that resentment that is carried to your grave or through your life. You must strive to be free of that to have free spirit, to have a spirit that is not tarnished in that sense.

It's a pretty big call to forgive.

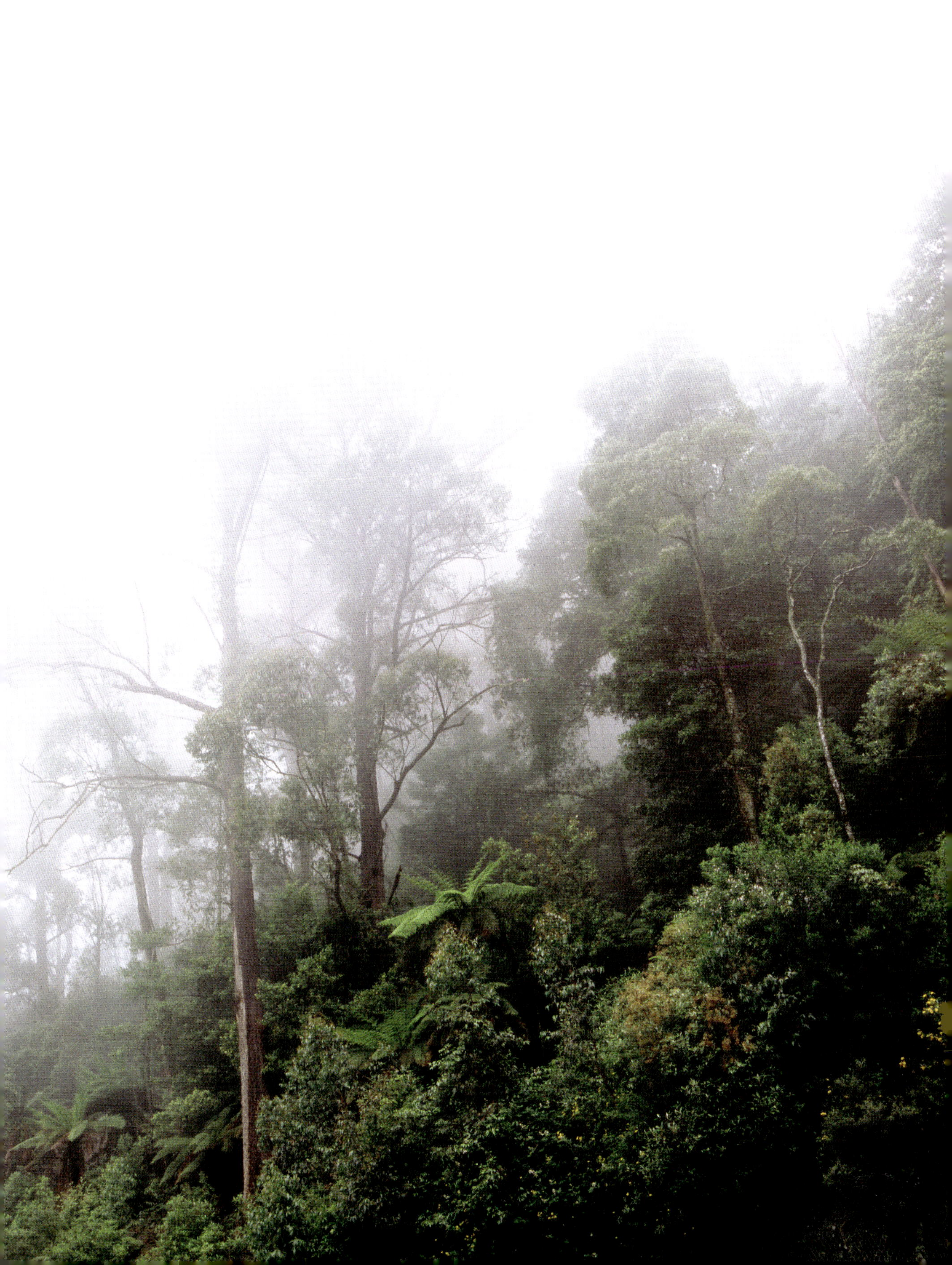

ACKNOWLEDGEMENTS

Thank you to my Elders, my grandfather and my Uncles for the knowledge handed to me. Thanks to my partner Marelle for her support. Thanks to Peter McConchie and my two grandsons who were with me on country for this book. Thanks to the National Parks and Wildlife Service, and the Aurthur Boyd Foundation for the accomodation in Shoalhaven.

Thanks to my mother for her spirit and for being with me on my journey throughout.

Max Dulumunmun Harrison

My People's Dreaming was recorded to celebrate the wisdom and teachings of Max Dulumunmun Harrison. A great deal of gratitude is extended to the team at Friends of the Earth (Melbourne) and People Culture Environment whose partnership in this project played an important role in bringing this story to us. To the Department of Environment and Climate Change (Narooma office) thank you for your care and understanding with our trip to Barran-guba Island. Thank you John Bennetts, Ron Cattell and David Prior for sharing Uncle Max's vision – you certainly got the project moving guys. And to the Architecture Foundation Australia, Peter Brock Foundation, The Bundanon Trust, Lesley Ann and Peter Marincowitz, The Rona Tranby Trust and Sydney Zen Centre, thank you for your support.

The photographs within this book were recorded with natural light using a Hasselblad 503cx and Nikon fm2 film cameras

Peter McConchie

Extensive text material in this book was supplied by Samantha Miles, editor at Finch Publishing, from her interviews with Uncle Max. Some further material was supplied with the kind permission of Dr Caroline Joseph, taken from her interviews with Uncle Max, published in the spring 2008 edition of 'Mind, Mood, Circle', the journal of the Sydney Zen Centre.

A note from Peter McConchie

As we search for a truer place in the world, Australian indigenous leadership offers many answers. To know more about Aboriginal people and how we can play a positive role in healing any remaining cultural divisions may also grant us access to a deeper connection to the natural world, spirituality and freedom.

Traditionally, Aboriginal culture is not written. For Max Dulumunmun Harrison's story to be presented in book form it has been recorded and transcribed from his homeland within the Yuin Nation. His words radiate a sense of connectedness to the earth and his traditional values are testimony to the oldest living culture on earth. The word 'Uncle' within indigenous culture is the name for teacher, relative, respected man or guardian. Uncle Max is a senior Elder of the Yuin Nation. He was born on the land beside a sacred water hole on the far South Coast of NSW and was chosen by his Elders to be taught traditional healing and medicine. This initial teaching spanned more than 15 years.

My first meeting with Uncle Max was during the recording of the book *Elders: Wisdom from Australian Indigenous Leaders*. I had sought Elders through National Indigenous Councils for the chapter on healing and Uncle Max was unanimously recommended. During my first meeting with Uncle Max I told him how I had found him through the National Councils and he replied, 'You think so, I have been singing someone up for years for this.' For me to attempt to describe how this book came about is now futile, as higher forces are obviously at work here. As as with *Elders*, the story had to be told.

The two young fellas that feature in some of the photographs are Uncle Max's grandsons, Max Dulumunmun Harrison III and Kyandle, the younger of the two. For the boys, recording *My People's Dreaming* was an important time to spend camping and travelling throughout their homeland, experiencing the teachings of their grandfather.

The diversity of landscapes represented in the photographs – from ancient forests, pristine rivers and rugged coastlines with ecosystems that support a bounty of life – shows the richness of Yuin country, which takes in and borders the coast south of Wollongong into Victoria, across to the Snowy River and up the Great Dividing Range.

My People's Dreaming speaks volumes in its direct delivery, contains wisdom that can be practised in our daily lives and gives us the opportunity to reinstate what is sacred.

Peter McConchie

My People's Dreaming: An Aboriginal Elder speaks on life, land, spirit and forgiveness.
First published in 2009 in Australia and New Zealand by Finch Publishing Pty Limited, ABN 49 057 285 248, Suite 2207, 4 Daydream Street, Warriewood, NSW, 2102, Australia.

12 11 10 09   8 7 6 5 4 3 2 1

Copyright © 2009 Max Dulumunmun Harrison, Peter McConchie and Finch Publishing

The authors assert their moral rights in this work throughout the world without waiver. All rights reserved. No part of this publication may be reproduced, stored in a retrieval system or transmitted in any form or by any means (electronic or mechanical, through reprography, digital transmission, recording or otherwise) without the prior written permission of the publisher.

All photographic images are by Peter McConchie, with the exception of those that appear on the following pages: page 100 courtesy of Stuart Cohen NSW National Parks and Wildlife Service; pages 16-31, 42, 70, 94 and 126 courtesy of Finch Publishing; page 86 courtesy of iStock International; page 123, young Aboriginal men with the Doonooch Dancers performing in the Woggan-ma-gule ceremony, Farm Cove, Royal Botanic Gardens, Sydney, on Australia Day 2009 courtesy of Finch Publishing.

National Library of Australia Cataloguing-in-Publication entry
Harrison, Max Dulumunmun.

My People's Dreaming : an Aboriginal Elder speaks on life, land, spirit and forgiveness /
Max Dulumunmun Harrison ; photographer Peter McConchie.

9781876451967 (hbk.)

Yuin (Australian people)--Philosophy.
Dreamtime (Aboriginal Australian mythology)--New South Wales--South Coast.

305.89915

Edited by Samantha Miles
Text designed and typeset by Creation Graphics
Cover design by Creation Graphics
Cover image courtesy of Peter McConchie
Print Management by Phoenix Offset
Printed in China

Reproduction and Communication for educational purposes
The Australian Copyright Act 1968 (the Act) allows a maximum of one chapter or 10% of the pages of this work, whichever is the greater, to be reproduced and/or communicated by any educational institution for its educational purposes provided that the educational institution (or the body that administers it) has given a remuneration notice to Copyright Agency Limited (CAL) under the Act. For details of the CAL licence for educational institutions contact: info@copyright.com.au

Finch titles can be viewed and purchased at **www.finch.com.au**

> **Note from the publisher**: There are many variations on the spelling of words within different Aboriginal languages. We have used the spellings of Aboriginal place names and spirits that best assist with correct pronunciation of these names. The term 'Uncle' is used to describe a man of wisdom and we have capitalised 'Uncle' to symbolise our respect for the role that an Uncle has in his community.
>
> Both the words 'lore' and 'law' are used throughout this book and have subtle differences in meaning. The term lore is used to suggest a set of customary practices, ways of living, storytelling and traditions. The word law refers to a body of rules that can be enforced. Within Yuin lore there are laws that can be enforced.